If Not Now, When?

By
Don O'Neal

Airleaf Publishing

airleaf.com

© Copyright 2006, Don O'Neal

All Rights Reserved.

No part of this book may be reproduced, stored in a retrieval system, or transmitted by any means, electronic, mechanical, photocopying, recording, or otherwise, without written permission from the author.

ISBN: 1-60002-275-8

To those who have made my life interesting, fun, and more fulfilling than I could have imagined: my mom and dad, Ed and Bertha O'Neal; my sisters and brothers and their spouses, Pat (Dave), Jean (Ernie), Joan (Don), Joye (Jim), John (Doris), Jeff, and Jerry; my children and their spouses, Cindy (Pete), Rhonda (Dave), and Brad (Becky), and their mother, Dolores; my stepdaughters and their spouses, Jennifer (Jeff), and Jill (John); my grandchildren, Neiman, Jeff, Eric, Jenna, Wil, Ellie, and Sydney; and especially Nancy, my wife and best friend.

TABLE OF CONTENTS

PREFACE.. ix

INTRODUCTION... xiii

PART I - BELIEVING 1

Chapter 1 - Why You <u>Should</u>.................................. 3
      - Dreamer #1
      - Dreamer #2
      - It's *Your* Future

      2 - Why You <u>Can</u>.. 16
           - Self-Confidence
           - Fear of Failure
           - It's What *You* Think That Matters

      3 - What You'll <u>Gain</u>.................................. 29
           - Motivation
           - Needs
           - Attitude

PART II - PLANNING... 41

Chapter 4 - Your <u>Dream</u> 43
      - Vision
      - Persistence

5 - Setting <u>Goals</u> 47
- *Which* Goals?
- *How Many* Goals?
- Measurable Goals
- Tradeoffs

6 - What You'll <u>Do</u> 56
- Actions
- Schedule
- Resources
- Control

7 - How You'll <u>Succeed</u> 63
- Initiative
- Persistence
- Focus

PART III - DOING 71

Chapter 8 - <u>Aiming High</u> 73
- Expectations 73

9 - <u>Looking Ahead</u> 81
- The Outside World
  - Uncertainty
  - Opportunities and Threats
  - Boundary Scanning
  - Inputs
  - Outputs

- You
    - Needs
    - Resources
    - Innovation

10 - How'm I Doin'? 99
- Feedback
- Stakeholders

11 - Changing 106
- Resisting Change
- Leading Change

PART IV - BECOMING 113

Chapter 12 - Self-Development 115
- Self-Assessment
- Setting Goals
- Job Identification

13 - Learning 122
- Knowledge
- Learning

14 - Character & Values 127
- Character
- Ethics
- Values

15 - Looking Back 133

PREFACE

"Someday, I'll...", "Someday, I'm going to...", "Someday." Sound familiar? How many times have you heard it? How many times have you *said* it?

I have a lot of interests, so there have always been things I've intended to do "someday." Some I have done, while others are still on my "someday" list, and every now and then, when I start to say, "someday, I'm going to...", my wife, an enthusiastic supporter of just about anything I want to do, quickly offers her standard challenge: "When?"

When I first mentioned that I was thinking about becoming a college professor "someday..." she asked, "How many more years do you think you have? If you don't do it now, when *will* you do it?" For some reason that question struck a chord that still resonates, and "If not now, when?" has become a mantra for me.

And it was that question that prodded me, a 50-something executive, to become a full-time doctoral student at a major university. When I left my job as a corporate vice president, my friends and colleagues were mystified. "How long will it take to earn your doctorate?" was often their first question, and when I responded, "about 5 years", they would invariably ask, "Do you know how *old* you'll be in five years?" Although I realized the question was rhetorical, my standard response was, "About the same age I'll be in five years if I *don't* do this."

Although I knew there would be many obstacles, foremost among them giving up a comfortable income for an uncertain future, once the decision was made I became so involved in my new life that I didn't have time for regrets, second-guessing myself, or worrying about the future.

The next few years were some of the most interesting and stimulating I've ever known, and by the time I completed my PhD and began my new career I *was*, sure enough, five years older, but in those five years I had begun living my dream. My new life as a college professor has been immensely satisfying, but it wouldn't have happened if I hadn't been prodded by the question, "If not now, when?"

It was that question that pried me out of my comfortable "rut" and made me take risks that I normally wouldn't have considered. As a result, I'm now a living example of Benjamin Franklin's observation, "The man who does what he loves will never work a day in his life."

I know there are many people who, like me, dream of things they'd like to do "someday" – a new job, a hobby, a business of their own, a long-delayed project, a trip to an exotic destination. But, for many, their dream may never be more than just a dream. Why? There may be a lot of reasons, but I think the most common are: they don't feel that they *should*; they don't believe that they *can*; they don't know *how*; or they can't seem to *get started* (just plain old inertia.) The purpose of this book is to help people get around, over, or through those barriers.

When we feel that we *shouldn't* do something, it is often because we feel guilty doing something for *ourselves.* It makes us seem selfish. I can't guarantee that I can help you feel unselfish about pursuing your dream, but I will show you that doing something for yourself is often the most *unselfish* thing you can do.

Then there's *can't,* one of the most disabling words in the English language. When we think we *can't* do something, it may be because we don't think we have everything we need (time, money, knowledge, skills, etc.) Although I can't give you time or money, I *can* show you ways to make the resources that you *have* go further than you might imagine.

And if you just don't have enough confidence in yourself or in your abilities, I will help you *learn how* to do whatever you want to do. Once you know *how,* it'll be easier to believe that you *can* make your dream come true. I'll lead you through a step-by-step process that will help you achieve just about anything you set your mind to. You supply the dream, and I'll walk you through a simple, logical, easy-to-understand process that will help you achieve it.

After you know *how,* you're ready for the most exciting step in making your dream a reality: *doing* it. To get started we first have to overcome *inertia*: our natural tendency to resist change; to stay where we are; to keep doing what we're doing. If we're sitting down, inertia makes it easier to stay there than to get up; if we're moving in a certain direction, our momentum (another form of inertia) makes it easier to keep going in that direction than to change direction.

Even if your life lacks excitement and variety, you aren't likely to change unless something forces you, and even then it may take something drastic, like the loss of a job, or a divorce. But I can help you find the incentive - the push you need to step out of your normal routine, and the energy to overcome inertia and pursue your dream – without waiting until something drastic happens. I'll do that by first, reassuring you that you *should*, second, convincing you that you *can*, third, helping you learn *how*, and finally, getting you *started*, and by the time you've completed this book, I'll bet that you, too, will be asking yourself, "If not now, when?"

INTRODUCTION

"You may not have been responsible for your heritage, but you are responsible for your future."
(Author unknown)

Each of us has a deep-seated need to be recognized and appreciated. We want to feel that what we are doing is worthwhile; that we are succeeding in our jobs and our lives; that what we do is important. This is true in our families, the organizations we belong to, and particularly in our jobs, where recognition is often associated with higher income and increased job security.

This book was written to help you address those needs: to help you become more successful in anything you do; to show you how to be better than just *good*; to help you achieve your fondest desires, your greatest aspirations, and get the recognition you deserve. It shows you how to do all that, not by working harder, but by becoming more *effective*.

Effectiveness does *not* come from working hard; it comes from getting *results*. To put it another way: just *doing* things won't make us successful, no matter how hard we work at them; we are only effective when we do the *right things*. But before we can do the right things, we have to know what they *are*, and that's where *planning* comes in.

Some people are content to take life as it comes, just letting life *happen,* as if everything was predetermined (some call it *fate*), with no particular plan for the future. They may feel they have no control over what happens to them; that their future will be determined *for* them, either by circumstances or by someone else, and that they have little choice but to live it the way it unfolds.

But life *isn't* like that; we don't have to live our lives that way. Our lives are *not* planned for us; we can plan the life we want, and make the future happen *our* way. Planning your life begins with a dream, a desire, an ambition, a vision: something so meaningful you're willing to plan, work, and sometimes sacrifice, to get it.

Your dreams are your hopes for the future; your aspirations; your long-range plans for what you want to do, or what you want to be. And dreams aren't just for dreaming; they don't have to be just wishes; they can come true. All it takes is for you to decide *what* you want and *how* to get it, then make up your mind to *do* it, and *believe* in yourself.

Once you've done that, the rest is pretty straightforward: you just focus your time and effort on doing exactly what you've planned. Of course it isn't as easy as I'm making it sound; it takes determination, commitment, and single-mindedness of purpose. But once you *believe* your dreams can come true, you unleash a powerful force: a vision that will help bring an intense focus to everything you do. That concentration will enable you to accomplish things that you might never have imagined.

The key is setting goals: determining what you have to do to achieve your vision. Once you've set goals, they become the driving force behind everything you do; every action you take, every effort.

Suppose, for example, you've dreamed of becoming an author. Can you do it? You can if you want to badly enough and if you're willing to work hard enough. How? First you have to find out what it takes to be an author; what knowledge, skills, and abilities are necessary. Now suppose you've done that, and you realize you'll need to improve your writing, and that the best way to do that is to complete your Journalism degree (the one you started but never finished.)

Then you find out which courses you'll need to take, and they become your first set of goals. Your course schedule becomes the center of your personal plan, and your vision is graduation. Your plan will keep your efforts focused on those goals and that vision – completing your degree. Nothing will be more important to you than finishing your studies. And your plan will be a roadmap you can use to monitor your progress: where you're going; what you have to do to get there; and where you are in the process, so you'll always know how you're doing.

Once you've graduated, you will have taken the first big step toward your dream. Then you ask yourself what's next?; what's the next step toward becoming an author? Perhaps you decide you should have some publishing experience, so you start searching for a job in publishing; that's your next goal. And that's how you achieve your dream, one step at a time, one goal at a time, never wasting your efforts on anything that doesn't help move you toward becoming an author.

And that's where this book comes in: it will *help you get the best results from your efforts; help you become more successful* in whatever you want to do.

It was written to help people like you be better than just good, at anything they do; to help you achieve whatever you desire. No matter who you are, where you are, or what you are doing right now, I can help you get the best results from your time and effort, both on and off the job. I'll show you how to reach your dreams, whatever they are; help you accomplish more than you ever thought you could.

I'll do that by helping you take charge of yourself, of what you do, and how you spend your time. I'll show you how to develop a personal plan, including a vision, specific goals, and clear-cut strategies for achieving those goals. And when you execute your plan you *will* be more successful in achieving whatever it is that you've chosen to do.

We all make choices about how to live our lives: we either look ahead and plan for our future, or sit back and let the future happen to us. The first option really is a choice, but the second is simply what happens when we *don't* make a choice.

If you take the second path, and just let your future *happen*, I can almost guarantee that you'll waste a lot of hard work, and maybe a lot of your life, bouncing from one situation to another, from one crisis to another, reacting to events and circumstances that you didn't see coming, simply because you didn't plan ahead.

But people who make their dreams come true don't take the future for granted; they make the future happen the way they want it to. This book was written to help you make *your* future happen – the future *you* want. After all,

"The future belongs to those who believe in the beauty of their dreams." (Eleanor Roosevelt)

If you'll let me help, we can turn your dream into reality and, in the process, start creating the future you want. I'll help you direct your time and effort toward the goals that are most important to you. You'll spend less time on "busy work," and on re-doing the same things you've always done, and more time on the things that really matter: those activities that will get you where you want to go. And you'll waste less time getting sidetracked by things that aren't really important.

How many times have you started a day with good intentions and a list of the things you wanted to accomplish, maybe even prioritized in order of their importance, and ended it exhausted from all you've done, but frustrated because you spent so much time working on things that weren't on your list?

That used to happen to me a lot: I can't count the times I left work feeling as though I hadn't accomplished anything, because I really *hadn't*; usually because I'd been detoured by things that "just came up"; items that would "only take a minute or two"; requests from people to whom I couldn't say "no"; and any number of other "things". And I'm not unusual; this happens to a lot of people, but I'm no longer one of them because I finally figured out how to avoid those situations.

I do it by *managing* myself, and everything I do, by priorities. I decide exactly which things are most important to me, and what I have to do to achieve them, then I don't let anything else get in the way.

Your personal plan can help you do the same thing: make sure your efforts are applied where they count the most. It's a simple process, but the results can have an enormous impact on your life and your career. Because, you see, no matter what you do, somebody is measuring your performance. Who? It could be any of a number of people, but let's assume that you work for a living and your boss is the one who measures your performance; the one who evaluates just how good you are.

It is a fact that our performance is measured by what we get done – by *results* – *not* by how hard we work. It's been my experience that most people work hard at what they do, but, as we've all seen, some people accomplish a lot more than others. What's the difference? I've found that those who accomplish the most do it by first making sure they're working on the *right* things, then concentrating on getting *those* things done, rather than anything else. I can help you be one of those people; the ones who get results.

This book is designed to help you manage yourself and any effort you undertake more effectively; to help you make the most effective use of your time and talents. It offers a step-by-step approach to better results by, first, helping you understand the power of focused efforts, then demonstrating how to invest the majority of your time and energy working toward specific goals, rather than wasting time working on things that don't really matter, or on fighting fires.

This book has been developed in four parts: Part I, *Believing*, Part II, *Planning*, Part III, *Doing*, and Part IV, *Becoming*.

Part I - Believing

This section discusses how to overcome some of the most common and most powerful barriers to individual success, most of which are based on our perceptions of ourselves, which are often wrong.

Chapter 1 discusses *why you should* follow your dreams and aspirations, not so much to convince you to *do* it, but to assure that you *deserve* to do it; that you have the *right* to do it.

Chapter 2 dispels the all-too-common misperception that we *can't* do something, which often comes from feelings of inadequacy: that we don't have the necessary time, money, knowledge, skills, or abilities.

Chapter 3 is about motivating yourself to *do something* about your dreams, to follow them, and *what you'll gain* when you do.

Part II - Planning

Personal planning begins with a *dream*, followed by a *vision* of how to make it a reality. Everything we do has a purpose, a reason, even though we don't always think about what that purpose is: *why* we're doing what we're doing. But we *should* think about it, because that's what gives *meaning* to our actions and, ultimately, to our lives. We should always have a clear picture of why we're doing something; what we're trying to achieve, and what actions are necessary to accomplish it.

The purpose of Chapter 4 is to describe and explain the process of developing a vision for reaching your dream.

Your vision happens one goal at a time. Each goal moves you one step closer to your vision and your dream. How to set goals, and which goals to set, are the subjects of Chapter 5.

The next step is deciding what you'll have to do to reach your goals: *what* needs to be done; *how* to do it; *when* it needs to be completed; and *who* will do it (if not you.) Chapter 6 leads you through the process of developing the *action plans* that will answer those questions.

And Chapter 7 focuses on the personal *commitment* that is absolutely essential to giving you the momentum and persistence to stay the course and succeed, no matter what obstacles or challenges you may encounter as you work toward your goals.

Part III - Doing

Now that you've completed the planning process, you're ready to put your plan into action.

Chapter 8 discusses the *expectations* – yours' and others' – that will be constant sources of both pressure and inspiration, as you put your plan into action.

Successful execution depends on having a good understanding of the *challenges* you're likely to face from the outside world; challenges that can become either opportunities or threats to your vision. Chapter 9 teaches you how to spot them, well in advance, and plan for how you'll deal with them.

Chapter 10 describes how to measure your progress against your plan; how to *evaluate* how you're doing at any time, so you can quickly make whatever changes may be necessary. Even the best plan can quickly become ineffective without ongoing feedback, evaluation and fine-tuning.

Chapter 11 discusses how to manage *change,* so it works *for* you rather than against you.

Part IV - Becoming

This section is all about you, and how you can develop the skills and abilities you need, learn what you need to know, and become the person you want to be.

Chapter 12 focuses on *self-development*; how to inventory your likes and dislikes, set personal goals, and find out which types of jobs or other pursuits will be most interesting, challenging, and rewarding for you.

Chapter 13 discusses the ways we *learn*, and how learning helps us acquire the knowledge that can make us outstanding at whatever we do.

Chapter 14 describes the importance of *character* to your success, and how to determine which values are most important to you.

Chapter 15 encourages you to look into the future and picture what you'd like to see when you sit back and *reflect* on your life: the things you did and didn't do.

Overview

Although the topics in this book are arranged in a linear sequence, it is important to recognize that the entire process, including believing, planning, and doing, is most effective as an iterative, or circular, process. Some activities, particularly those involving some trial and error, can begin early in the process, even before your plan has been fully developed. This will provide early feedback on how well your plan is working, so you can make improvements as you go along.

PART I

BELIEVING

The most important ingredient in making your dreams, your hopes, your desires become reality is *you*. Until you have a clear understanding of what you want and why you want it, and even more important, what's keeping you from getting it, it's likely to be difficult, if not impossible, for you to get it. But I'm going to help you get there, beginning with a better understanding of what makes you tick, or perhaps *not* tick.

The chapters in this section focus on helping you believe that you *should* reach for your dreams, that you *can* do it, and what you'll *gain* from the process.

CHAPTER 1 - WHY YOU <u>SHOULD</u>

"For all sad words of tongue or pen,
the saddest of these: 'It might have been!'"
(John Greenleaf Whittier, 1807-1892)

You've seen them, I've seen them; those people we all admire who can decide they want to do something and, before you know it, they've done it.

Like the person who leaves a secure job with a successful company to start his own business, with all the risk and hard work it entails. Did he consciously decide that he *should*, and *could*, and did he understand all he had to *gain*, then lay out a formal plan for *how* to do it?

Or the one who divorces while in her forties, then plans and oversees construction of a smaller home that's just right for her new circumstances.

Another takes years to finish a long-abandoned degree, while working full time, then takes early retirement to work toward a master's degree in an entirely new field.

These are people who had dreams, and decided to do something about them. They felt like they *should*, believed they *could*, and knew what they had to *gain*, so they figured out *how* to get what they wanted.

Are these inspiring people extraordinary? Not necessarily. None of them were born rich, nor did they "get the breaks." They're just like you and me, except that they've learned the power of focusing their efforts on achieving their goals. It may not be something they've always known how to do, but they certainly do now.

Of course we all know the great success stories, like Andrew Carnegie, John D. Rockefeller, Sam Walton, and Bill Gates, but we're going to focus on people, like those you know personally, who have enriched their lives in great measure, or in small but meaningful ways: those who've done it by actually *working* toward their dreams, rather than sitting idly by, thinking "Wouldn't it be great if someday...?" Think about them, then think about yourself. Isn't there something you've always wanted to do?

Of course there is, so come along and let me help you get it done. But first, let me tell you about two dreamers; two ordinary dreamers, and what they did to make their dreams come true; two stories that may help convince you why *you* should follow *your* dreams.

Dreamer #1

As far back as he could remember, he had dreamed of things he wanted, but this dream was different. Somehow it lit a fire in him and became his driving passion – the inspiration for everything he did. He was 12 or 13, maybe 14, when he first learned about West Point. The United States Military Academy, at West Point, New York had, for more than 150 years, been an incubator of heros; the training ground of many of America's greatest military leaders: Grant, Lee, Pershing, MacArthur, Eisenhower, Patton, and many

If Not Now, When?

others. Something about it struck a chord, and West Point became his dream.

He read about it; everything he could get his hands on: its history, rules and regulations, catalogs and admission requirements. Not only did he become an expert on the subject, he also made a decision, years before he would be old enough to attend, that one day he would be a West Pointer. And from that point on he didn't just dream about it, he did something about it. Nothing was going to stand in his way. He was going to get there, one way or another. And he became the personification of determination.

Beginning his first year in high school, he selected his classes with West Point in mind. A foreign language was an entrance requirement, so he struggled through two years of French. Proficiency in mathematics was essential, so he took all the math courses he could get, including the highest levels offered at his school. Physical conditioning and participation in team sports was considered important, so he went out for basketball, baseball, and track, the only sports his small school offered. He wasn't a natural athlete but, determined to be as good as he possibly could, through hard work and persistence he became a mainstay on his school teams.

Everything he did during high school was geared toward West Point: he dreamed it, lived it, and wasn't hesitant to tell everybody about it, and about his determination to get there. He was painting a mental picture of his future, and doing everything he could to make it come true.

And his efforts began to pay off. By the end of his Junior year, there was no question that he would be able to meet all of the entrance requirements, both academic and physical. So he had overcome the first obstacles, but there was another yet to come, one that would turn out to be even more difficult.

Admission to West Point was by appointment only, and most appointments were in the hands of United States Senators and Congressmen. Even a candidate who had met all of the admission requirements couldn't be admitted without an appointment, Unfortunately, living in a rural area hadn't given our dreamer much visibility with his elected representatives, and he didn't know anybody who could help him gain access to them. And when he finally realized that even writing letters wouldn't get him a congressioinal appointment, he decided to try his only remaining avenue: a *competitive* appointment.

But there were very few competitive appointments each year, and they were only available to active members of the armed forces, or armed forces reserves. So, when he reached his 17th birthday, although he was just finishing his junior year in high school, our dreamer joined the National Guard. By the time he graduated from high school, the following year, he had completed his first year of service, which made him eligible to take the competitive exam for West Point.

Unfortunately, the competitive exam was given only once each year, in March, so he would have to wait until the next year to take it. Undeterred, he

If Not Now, When?

enrolled in college that fall, to keep his academic skills honed.

The next spring he took the competitive exam: three days of intensive written and physical tests, followed by an exhaustive medical examination.

Several weeks later he received word that he had done very well. He had placed 2nd among more than 900 applicants but, unfortunately, only one competitive appointment was available. Although deeply disappointed, he was somewhat encouraged by one official, who urged him to try again the following year, with the assurance that if he did as well as this year, there would definitely be an appointment available for him.

So back to college he went, to make sure he didn't lose his edge, and the next year he tried again; same time of the year, same place, same tests, and the same excruciating wait for the results.

But this time he received the word that he had hoped for: he was in. He was ordered to report to West Point for induction that July, a full two years after his high school graduation, and at least six years after he had first put his plan into action.

So, that July he began Plebe year, the most challenging phase of West Point. It's a year of probation; of proving yourself; a full year of intense academic and physical challenges, while under constant hazing and harassment by upperclassmen. But he had read so much about it that he knew how it would be, and he was prepared to handle it, both physically and mentally.

And he *did* handle it, so when the next June finally rolled around, he ended his Plebe year by proudly marching in the Graduation Parade and being formally "recognized" by the upperclassmen. Recognition meant that he was now a third classman – a Yearling. He had done it! He had completed his probationary year, and was now a full-fledged West Pointer.

The next day he left for home, on his first leave in almost a year. And he never returned to West Point...Why? The reason doesn't matter – it made sense at the time – what matters is that he had his dream in his hands – the dream he had worked so long and so hard for – and he let it go.

Dreamer #2

It's surprising how guilty we can feel just *thinking* about doing something for ourselves. It's almost as though we believe that everything we do should be for *others*; that it's selfish to do something just because *we* want to.

I have a friend who has always justified doing something for himself by saying "I owe it to myself." For the longest time I viewed that as merely a way of rationalizing selfish behavior, but I've since come to the conclusion that there can sometimes be real value in looking at things his way.

When I was young my goals, though generally honorable, were mostly self-serving: have fun, participate in sports, earn some money, get an education, enjoy my friends, and search for that special young lady. They were mostly about *me*. But as I

If Not Now, When?

matured, a sense of duty, of responsibility took over; first to my family, but also to my friends, community, and employer. Of course getting married had a lot to do with that; almost overnight my goals became family-oriented: a wife, children, and a career that would enable me to give them everything I thought they should have. So it was no longer about me, it was now about others; about being a husband, father, and provider. But I enjoyed it, and the years flew by, until suddenly (or so it seemed) our children were all grown and gone, and something felt different.

I still had responsibilities, still worked for a living, but with the kids gone it seemed as though I had a lot less responsibility, or maybe it was that my responsibilities didn't seem as pressing. In any event, after so many years as a protector and provider, I started to think again about me: "Who am I, really? Who do I want to be?" Natural questions, I suppose, since so much of our self-concept, self-esteem, and self-worth depends on what we feel we've accomplished.

We all have a need to feel good about ourselves and to have others respect us. A lot of our self-esteem comes from achievement, and from the recognition and appreciation that are part of what we accomplish. Because self-esteem gives us the confidence to face the world, building and maintaining it is important to our success in whatever we do. Our self-esteem is closely tied to our performance: it rises and falls depending on what we expect of ourselves and how well we meet those expectations. It comes from what we do, and how well we do it.

But even when our self-esteem is high – when we're confident and assured of our own value – we may become restless and discontented if we're not getting enough *satisfaction* from what we do. This is our need for self-actualization. To be truly happy a person *must* be what he or she *can* be: "A musician must make music, an artist must paint, a poet must write, if he is to be ultimately at peace with himself" (Maslow,1998:3) But when we feel that we're not realizing our full potential – not doing as well as we should be doing, or not being the person we think we could be – it is likely to affect our self-esteem, in a negative way.

And that's where I found myself at that point in my life. Although I enjoyed my profession, and had been very successful, I started to question what I was accomplishing through my work, besides earning a living: "Am I doing all I'm capable of? What would I really enjoy doing? What would give me the most satisfaction? Am I who I want to be?" Actually, I didn't even *know* who I wanted to be.

About that time I saw an advertisement for an Executive MBA program, and was able to convince my company to sponsor me. The program offered weekend classes for business executives who are full-time employees, and it required two years of intensive study to earn a Masters Degree in Business Administration.

Being a full-time graduate student while still working full time was challenging, but I thrived on it because it was stimulating! It made me think, question, challenge and, most of all, learn. And almost immediately I sensed an increase in my self-confidence,

If Not Now, When?

which is particularly interesting because I had never felt a *lack* of confidence. But apparently my self-esteem wasn't as strong as it could have been, perhaps because what I had been doing wasn't particularly satisfying; I wasn't yet who I wanted to be.

As I watched my professors in action and got to know them better, I could see that these were people who really enjoyed what they were doing. They were good at it, and they knew it. I began to picture myself in that role: helping people learn how to be more successful in life. I had done a lot of training in my business career, so I was confident of my teaching abilities, and I could remember so well the satisfaction of helping someone grasp an idea; seeing their eyes light up when they understood.

So, midway through the MBA program, I began exploring what I would have to do to become a professor. One of the first things I learned was that most colleges and universities preferred their professors to have doctoral degrees, and many required them. So before I could become a professor I would have to earn a doctorate – a long and difficult process.

So began my internal tug of war: "Should I study for a doctorate or not?" It would require becoming a full-time student (not just weekends), which would mean leaving my job as a corporate vice-president. Note that I said "*should* I…", not *could* I, because by this time I was confident that, if I could succeed in the MBA program, I could succeed at anything. However, there was a financial concern – could I afford it?

Financial feasability was simply a matter of budget – did I have enough financial resources to see me through at least 2 ½ years without any other income? All it took to answer that question was a spread-sheet of my estimated living expenses for the next 2 ½ years. When it became clear that my savings would just (barely) cover my expenses for that length of time, the question of *could* was resolved.

But *should I* was also a financial issue, because it involved my sense of responsibility: "To whom am I responsible for how I spend my savings? Do I owe it to my children to be self-supporting in my later years, so they won't have to worry about taking care of me? Do I owe it to them to have something left to leave them after I'm gone – an inheritance?"

And that's where my friend's self-serving statement, "I owe it to myself," once again came to mind. As I questioned whether or not it would be fair to spend my savings on more education, I also asked: "What's fair for me? What do I owe myself? Which will make me happier, continuing to do what I'm doing, or doing what I *want* to do?" The answer to that one was never in doubt.

By now you know the outcome: I was selfish; I put myself first; I finally convinced myself that I owed it to myself; and I decided that I *should*. The result? It's been everything I had imagined, and more. I've been teaching for more than a decade now, well past the age at which I would have retired from my previous job, and I'm happier and healthier than I've ever been. My family? They're enjoying it as much as I am. Seeing

If Not Now, When?

me enjoy what I do has been uplifting for them. And the money? That's never been an issue for them. In fact, my son, who was still in college when I became a PhD student, proudly displayed a home-made bumper-sticker that said "My Dad and My Inheritance go to the University of Illinois"

Finally getting to do what *I* wanted required overcoming many obstacles, but the most difficult was convincing myself that I had the right to do it; that I *should*. I imagine that was because, after so many years of feeling that my responsibility was to others, it seemed selfish to put my own desires first. But it was worth it. The *me* that I am today is much happier and more satisfied than the person I was then. And there's no question that the risk I took in being "selfish" has paid great dividends, not only for me, but also for everyone close to me.

But what about Dreamer #1? Whatever happened to him? Did he regret his decision?

As a matter of fact, for years he didn't even think about it. Perhaps because he was too busy; too involved in other things. Or maybe he just wouldn't *let* himself think about it. But one day he did think about it, and began wondering what might have been. If he could do it over again would he do it differently?

Well, he wisely decided to not even try answering that question; he knew he *couldn't* recapture that dream, even if he wanted to. There are some dreams that you can let go and later come back to, even a long time later, but this wasn't one of them; there was no going back.

But the fact that he had let one dream slip away made him more determined not to let it happen again. There would be other dreams and, one by one, he worked to make them come true, but always with one thought in mind – he wouldn't ever let another one get away.

By now you may have guessed that the West Pointer and the professor are one and the same. Letting go of that one dream affected my entire life, but fortunately in a very positive way, even though I didn't realize it for a long time. Everything that I've done since West Point has probably, in some way, been influenced by my determination to achieve whatever I set out to do, to finish what I start, and to continue to follow my dreams.

It's *Your* Future

We have a choice in how we approach our future, generally viewing it in one of two ways: activity, or expectation.

Through *activity* we can move toward the future, creating it as we go. If we choose *expectation*, we will wait for the future to come to us. The choice is ours, but it's important to consider the risk attached to waiting. Allen Bluedorn warns us, "…when procrastination results in a task or project never attempted, in a path never taken, the consequences can last a lifetime. And from the standpoint of the individual psyche, a major consequence is often regret…Research…found that the things people regret

If Not Now, When?

the most in their lives tend to be the things they decided not to do, the errors of omission." (2002:239,240)

So think about it. Do you want to spend the rest of your life looking back with regret at the things you *didn't* do? Isn't it about time to ask yourself, "Shouldn't I do something for myself; be who *I* want to be?"? Why not take a peek into your future and visualize what life will be like if you do what you've always wanted to do; be the person you always knew you could be? Then give yourself permission; reassure yourself that you have a right to do it; that you *should* do it. After all, *if not now, when?*

Now, on to the next chapter, and the assurance that you *can*.

CHAPTER 2 - WHY YOU <u>CAN</u>

"A strong passion for any object will ensure success,
for the desire of the end will point out the means."
(William Hazlitt, 1778-1830)

"If you care enough for a result,
you will most certainly attain it."
(William James, 1842-1910)

Now that you know that you have a right, even a responsibility, to follow your dreams, the next step is convincing yourself that you *can*. For some people that's harder than convincing themselves that they *should*. Why? There are a variety of reasons, some more common than others.

Self-Confidence
Perhaps the most obvious, and certainly one of the most powerful reasons that people don't follow their dreams is that they don't have confidence in themselves: they don't believe they can do it. Maybe it's because a task this size seems overwhelming; especially if you've never attempted anything like this before, anything this big.

Or maybe you don't feel you have the knowledge, or the skills, or the time, or the money. Any of these reasons can seem insurmountable, but believe it or not, all of them can be overcome.

If Not Now, When?

Lack of ability is seldom the reason people can't make things happen; more often it's a state of mind: they just don't *believe* they can. But it's amazing what people can do when they set their minds to it and, and even more important, when they *believe* they can. I have long been fascinated by books on that subject – the power of the human mind – and I'd like to tell you about four of them, because of the way they have influenced my thinking.

I have long since forgotten how I came across *The Magic of Believing*, but it was my first exposure to the power of believing in myself. We can do just about anything that we *believe* we can. This book was written by a businessman, Claude Bristol, who discusses the power that exists in our subconscious minds, and demonstrates how to use that power. Like many people, I was skeptical of anything I couldn't *see*, anything that looked like witchcraft or hocus-pocus, but this author's ideas fascinated me, because they seemed to explain some things that had mystified me; things I had never really understood.

For example, when I first read his book I was a practicing engineer who had long been intrigued by the fact that some of my best ideas, and the solutions to some of my toughest problems, came to me early in the morning, often while taking my morning walk or in the shower. I assumed this was happening because I was fresher and more clear-headed early in the day, but as I read more about the subconscious mind – that our subconscious memory is believed to retain everything we have ever heard, seen, read about, or experienced – I began considering the possibility that my early-morning revelations may have been my subconscious memory at work.

It is undoubtedly true for many professions, but I know it's a fact for engineers: the more experience you have, the more information you can draw on, and the better you become as an engineer. But, unfortunately, a lot of the information and knowledge that we gain from experience isn't readily available to us; it isn't at our fingertips; we've forgotten a lot of it; perhaps most of it. Why? Research has shown that our *short-term* memory can only hold a few pieces of information at a time, and once it's full any new information that comes in replaces some of the previous information. But the information that's pushed out isn't really lost; it stays in our *subconscious* memory, which never forgets *anything*. While it's reassuring to know that everything we've ever learned is in there somewhere, recalling something we need, precisely when we need it, doesn't seem possible. But Claude Bristol assures us it *is* possible; that we can utilize our subconscious memories, almost at will.

So I decided to test his ideas by deliberately trying to draw on my subconscious to get new ideas and to solve problems. I began to practice, just before going to sleep at night, concentrating on a particular problem. I would focus intently on it for a few minutes, not trying to solve it, just trying to embed it in my mind. What happened?

Did it work? Yes it did, and although most of the time I used it for work-related issues, it worked just as

If Not Now, When?

well for personal and financial issues. Did it always work? Not every time, but often enough to convince me that any time I wasn't deliberately calling on my subconscious to help me, I was wasting a powerful force. And as I used it, I remembered an incident from my childhood.

One night, as I was getting ready for bed, I told my mother I was worried that I wouldn't wake up in time to go on a class field trip, which was leaving at 4:30 in the morning. Mom assured me that she wouldn't let me oversleep, but suggested that I could wake *myself* up, using a method that had always worked for her. I decided to try and, just before going to sleep, concentrated for a few minutes on a single thought: waking up at 4:00. And what do you know? It worked! I actually woke up a few minutes before mom called me, and was so impressed with that method that I used it occasionally over the years, although I really didn't understand *why* it worked until I read Bristol's book.

That simple system can work the same way for you. You, too, have a wonderful subconscious store of information that you can use to help overcome obstacles and solve problems. Why not try it?

Another book that had a big influence on me was *The Quick and Easy Way to Public Speaking*, written by Dale Carnegie, a teacher. Its purpose was to help people overcome their fear of public speaking. It has been said that of all the things people fear, the only thing that terrifies us more than the thought of speaking in front of others is the fear of death. Many people feel that they just can't speak in front of an audience. But

Don O'Neal

Carnegie found a way to give people confidence that they *could* speak in front of others, by teaching them three rules: 1) talk only about something you *know well*; 2) make sure your subject is something you're excited about; and 3) be eager to share what you know about the subject.

Please understand, I'm not suggesting that you become a public speaker, but I know that at least two of Carnegie's rules apply to pursuing your dreams: 1) knowing a lot about something; and 2) being excited about it. If it's your dream, your fondest desire, you *will* know a lot about it; and your interest will make it *exciting* for you; and if you're excited about it, you *will* find a way to do it. It's that simple (well, almost.)

The third book is *The Power of Positive Thinking*, written by Dr. Norman Vincent Peale, a minister, to help people build self-confidence, was called by its publisher "The Greatest Inspirational Bestseller of Our Time." Dr. Peale taught people to believe in themselves, mentally picture what they want to achieve, and drive out negative thinking by replacing every negative thought with one that's positive. And it works. Why? Buddha explains it:

"All that we are is the result of what we have thought. The mind is everything. What we think, we become."

Our thinking influences us in two ways: positively, to help reinforce the belief that we *can*, or negatively, to reinforce our belief that we *can't*. But negative thinking only works *against* us; it discourages us and saps our energy. So Dr. Peale suggests that whenever

If Not Now, When?

we start thinking negatively we should deliberately replace the negative thought with something positive. Replace "I can't", or "I don't think I can" with "*How can I?*" Try it. It works wonders.

By coincidence, Dale Carnegie, when asked the most important lesson he had ever learned, replied, "...the stupendous importance of what we think...for your thoughts make you what you are. By changing our thoughts, we can change our lives." (1965:16) Sounds like a testimonial to Dr. Peale's book, doesn't it?

The fourth book, *Jonathon Livingston Seagull*, written by Richard Bach, an aviator, has become a classic about thinking differently; achieving what nobody else thinks you *can*; doing what nobody else thinks you *should*; being *different* from those around you; and most of all, having a dream and making it come true. For me, this book is a constant reminder that what somebody else thinks you *can't* do isn't important at all; the only thing that matters is what you believe you *can* do.

Of course these books are just a small sample of the many authors whose thoughts have made an impression on me, but they are at the top of my list because they provide evidence that, in spite of what anybody else thinks, we are capable of doing just about anything we set our minds to; that we *can* if we will only *believe* that we can.

Fear of Failure

Another barrier to believing that we *can* is the fear of failing; worrying that there'll be a stigma attached if we try something and don't succeed: that others may see us as "losers." We all have this fear to some degree. With it comes a fear that failing will hurt our self-confidence; make us more insecure; make us *feel* like failures; make us see *ourselves* as losers. Or fear of failure may come from our concern about what *others* will think of us. We worry about what *they* will say: those who don't think we *should*, and those who don't think we *can*. Can't you almost hear them saying "I told you so!"?

Our fear of failure may be reinforced by the way our on-the-job performance is evaluated. Many organizations view as failure anything we try that doesn't work; anything new that doesn't succeed the first time. Viewed that way, people who try something that doesn't work are likely to be seen as incompetent, or less competent than their co-workers, the ones who never make mistakes (maybe because they never try anything new.)

Of course there is a sure way to avoid failure: never try anything new; never do anything that you haven't done before. What if athletes looked at it that way? In baseball, for example, even the greatest hitters of all time failed more times than they succeeded. Think about it: even a .300 hitter fails to hit 70% of the time, and Babe Ruth, one of the most famous home-run hitters of all time, struck out more often than any other player; he failed more often than he succeeded. As somebody once said "You miss 100% of the shots that you don't take."

This means, of course, that if you don't try you'll never fail, but what's more important is that if you don't try you have *no chance to succeed.* Picture yourself someday looking back and thinking, "Well, I never failed, but then again I didn't even *try* to follow my dream." Not a very comforting thought is it?

It's What *You* Think That Matters

A final thought on believing: sometimes the feeling that we can't do something is strongly influenced by the perceptions of others. Everyone who knows us has an image of us; of what we are to them. If they're close to us, they're probably comfortable with who we *are* (or who *they* think we are), and they'd prefer that we stay that way; it keeps the relationship predictable. The thought of change scares those who are close to us. They don't want another us, and they'll go to great lengths to convince us that we can't change, or that we *shouldn't.*

This was the dilemma of Jonathon Livingston Seagull: seagulls don't do the things that Jonathon was doing; to the other seagulls the most important part of flying was to get from the shore to their food source and back again; a means of transportation. But for Jonathon, flying was everything. How the other seagulls viewed Jonathon's obsession was best expressed by his mother, when she asked "Why, Jon, *why*? Why is it so hard to be like the rest of the flock, Jon? Why can't you leave low flying to the pelicans, the albatross? Why don't you *eat*?" (1970:13) Jon's response was typical of dreamers, of believers, "I just want to know what I can do in the air and what I can't, that's all. I just want to know."(1970:14)

And Jonathon's mother was just doing what those around us often do; they remind us of who we are, or who *they* think we should be, by saying something that sounds an awful lot like "Why aren't you content being like the rest of the flock?" So don't be surprised when you're asked those questions, and don't be afraid to answer, "Because I don't *want* to be like the rest of the flock". Now, before we move on, let me share with you another example of someone who didn't want to be like the rest of the flock: not a seagull, but a real live person.

On the surface, everything about Dave was ordinary, average; nothing about him appeared outstanding or unusual. He was born into a large family—not uncommon in the 1930s—in a small Midwestern town. His were working-class parents, who instilled in their children a sense of responsibility and a strong work ethic, neither of which was unusual in those days. And, as in most working families, although they never lacked for food, housing or love, there was seldom money for non-essentials. So Dave, like his brothers and sisters, knew that any spending money would have to come from their own resourcefulness.

Fortunately, Dave wasn't lazy, and learned that there were plenty of opportunities for a young boy to earn extra money, by mowing lawns, shoveling snow, or stocking shelves in a grocery store, to name just a

If Not Now, When?

few. Of course he had competition – his friends and siblings had to earn their own spending money, too – but Dave quickly learned something that most of his competitors didn't: the value of customer service. Dave wasn't just willing to work; he was conscientious about his work. He didn't just do the work and collect his money; he took pride in doing a good job, and his customers soon learned that although he might charge the same price as others, the quality of his work was better. It was the best. The result? New customers, referred by old customers, came to him – he didn't have to go looking for them – so he always had plenty of opportunities to make money. So at least in this one way, Dave wasn't ordinary, after all—he was extraordinary! But many would say this single advantage was more than offset by a huge personal disadvantage.

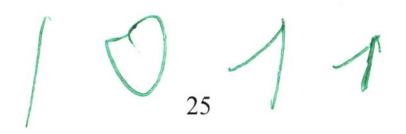

You see, as a student Dave was, to put it kindly, below-average. He just didn't like school; it was a challenge for him, undoubtedly because of his stuttering. So most of the time he just listened, except, that is, when he was called on to recite in class, and you can just about imagine how the other kids made fun of his awkward attempts to get his words out. So, as a student, Dave failed three times; he had to repeat three grades. Yet, he didn't drop out; he kept coming back, although it meant he wouldn't finish high school until he was 21 years old—three years late. But the important thing is that he *did* graduate. Dave wasn't a quitter, which is quite remarkable considering how frustrating it must have been to be considered "slow." He knew it; and realized that *everyone* in town knew it.

But Dave knew that he was anything but ordinary. Dave *believed in himself*; he knew what he was capable of, and he was a dreamer. Dave dreamed big; but he was also realistic. He knew the world wouldn't be beating a path to his door when he graduated from high school; he knew that he wouldn't only have to find a job, he'd also have to sell himself, to convince an employer to overlook his stuttering. To many, this would have been too big a barrier to overcome, but Dave wasn't intimidated by barriers; he had already overcome too many. Because you see, his conscientious approach to work – any work that he did – had not only impressed his customers, it had also built his confidence. By now, Dave was convinced that he could accomplish anything.

His first jobs were working for others, but Dave never lost sight of his dream to have a business of his own, and before long he *did* own a business of his own, and then another and a third. Now you'd think that a young man who has overcome all that Dave had, and now owned three successful businesses, would slow down and rest on his laurels, but that wasn't Dave; he was on a path to a bigger dream.

Because Dave's small town was typical of many in the midwest during the last half of the twentieth century; it was slowly dying. As young people graduated from high school they moved away to areas that offered better job opportunities. But Dave had a vision of bringing people back to the area, and one day

If Not Now, When?

found what he thought might be the way: making baskets. His small town had once been a basketmaking center, but the business had died out long ago. His grandfather had been a basketmaker, and Dave's father had become an expert at the trade, but only part time, as a way to make extra money, not as a profession.

Dave envisioned his father making baskets and he, Dave, selling them. But his vision wasn't limited to a small basket-making business; he saw this as a way to re-start an industry; one that would not only create jobs for local people, but one that would ultimately develop his town as a tourist attraction. Of course, any time he mentioned his grandiose vision to anyone else, including his family, people would just shake their heads. Here was a guy who almost didn't make it through high school; what chance would he have to develop a vision like that? Well, guess what?

Dave's dream came true. Did I mention Dave's last name? It was Longaberger, and Longaberger Baskets are known around the world. The company is a $1 billion business employing 8000 people, and the small town of Dresden, Ohio welcomes hundreds of thousands of visitors every year. Isn't that something? And all because Dave Longaberger wouldn't let the fact that he stuttered, and was considered a slow learner, keep him from following his dreams.

Of course, your dream may not be as big as Dave's, and it doesn't have to be. But if he could overcome his obstacles and change the destiny of an entire area, surely you have what it takes to make *your* dream a reality.

The whole point of this chapter has been to help you believe that you *can* do whatever you want, if you *believe* you can do it, and if you want to do it badly enough. *I* believe you can, but if you're not yet convinced, maybe you need a bit more encouragement; an incentive. So let's go to the next chapter and talk about what you'll *gain* by following your dreams.

CHAPTER 3 - WHAT YOU'LL *GAIN*

> "The only happy people I know
> are the ones who are working well
> at something they consider important."
> (Abraham Maslow, 1908-1970)

What do *you* want out of life? What do you think about and wish for? What are your hopes and dreams? Have you ever really thought about it?

I do, every now and then, and I'm sure a lot of other people do, too; maybe most of us. But many of those who *think* about what they want never *do* anything about it. They don't do what it takes to stop wanting and start having. Why not? While there may be a lot of reasons, it all really comes down to *motivation*. Motivation is almost always the difference between those who get what they want and those who don't.

Motivation

Everything we desire is driven by some *need* that we have. We want it because it will *do* something for us, or it will give us satisfaction, or for how it will make us feel. The desire to satisfy those needs—to achieve our hopes and dreams—can be a powerful motivator, if we let it.

We hear a lot about motivation, "She's motivated," "He's not motivated," and there's the "motivated seller," a big catch-phrase in real estate, which means that the owner of a property has a strong desire/need to sell it.

People who achieve their dreams are usually highly motivated: they want them so badly they'll do whatever it takes to get there. How do they get that motivated? More importantly, how can *you* get motivated like them?

First, you have to know what will motivate you: what will drive you to take action; to *do* something. Then you have to understand that all motivation is self-induced. You have to motivate yourself; nobody else can do that for you.

If you want something badly enough, you'll do whatever it takes to get it. That's motivation. On the other hand, the only way that *I* could get you to do something would be to find a way to make you *want* to do it. That means that even if you do something that somebody else wants you to, you'll only do it if it will get you something that *you* want.

For example, the best students are usually those who enjoy their studies, and are in school not just because they *have* to be, but because they *want* to be. Other students are only in school because somebody else (e.g., their parents, the law) *requires* them to be there, so they are less motivated and more likely to be average or below-average in their studies. This difference is particularly noticeable in college students.

It's been said that everything we do is either to experience pleasure or to avoid pain. If that's true, that means we won't do anything unless it will gain us something of value, or let us avoid something

If Not Now, When?

unpleasant or undesirable. In any event, we are all more likely to take action when it has some personal benefit because, to some degree, we're all driven by the unspoken question, "What's in it for me?" That's motivation.

So doesn't it make sense to ask ourselves what *are* the things that we really would like to have, or do? Even better, what are the things that *excite* us? Because those are the keys to motivating ourselves. We need to know exactly what we want most. Now, that might sound like a statement of the obvious, but strange as it may seem, some people don't know themselves very well; I mean *really* know themselves. And that may be because they just don't take the time to think about themselves.

That's understandable, if we consider the time and energy it takes just to cope with the day-to-day challenges of our lives; meeting our obligations to our families and to our jobs. These challenges are so all-consuming they can easily overshadow everything else, leaving little time for the luxury of thinking about the future, or reflecting on our hopes and dreams.

So if we want to think about our own needs, the things we really want, we have to *make* time. We have to stand up and ask ourselves "Don't I owe it to myself?" then have the courage to answer back, loud and clear, "Yes, I do!"

So one of the first steps in pursuing your dreams is getting them out of the shadows; bringing them out into the light; giving them the attention they deserve. Only then can you sort out your needs; determine which are really important, and which are merely short-term distractions.

Needs

Abraham Maslow, a psychologist, recognized that each of us has a variety of needs, which we prioritize in the order of their importance. Sometimes we consciously rank our needs, but probably more often we do it unconsciously, automatically, without even thinking about it. At any given time, our most urgent needs will dominate our thoughts and actions, at least until they have been satisfied, and until they have we won't think about much else. But every time one need is satisfied another will take its place, and we'll shift our attention to it until it's been satisfied, and so on.

Maslow suggested that we have five levels of needs, beginning with the lowest level - our most basic needs - which he termed *physiological* needs. Physiological needs include the need for food, water, and reproduction. Until our physiological needs have been satisfied we won't care about anything else, because they are absolutely essential to our survival: we need food and water to survive from day to day, and reproduction for the human race to survive. But once our physiological needs have been satisfied, another kind of need becomes more important to us: *safety*.

Examples of our safety needs include protection from the elements (a roof over our heads), and from harm (disease, illness, accidents, enemies.) As long as we have concerns for our safety, any higher-order needs are relatively unimportant, but once we're free from

If Not Now, When?

safety concerns, the next higher level of needs, *love*, becomes most important.

Sometimes referred to as social needs, our love needs include the need for love, affection, and belonging. Until they've been met we are likely to be obsessed with making friends, finding a mate, and perhaps having children. And only when our love needs have been met will we move to the next level, *esteem*.

Esteem needs include the need to feel good about ourselves: for self-esteem and self-respect; to be appreciated and recognized for our accomplishments. Our desire for esteem may never be *completely* satisfied, we can always use additional reassurance, but when it has been reasonably satisfied, our highest level need comes into play - the need for *self-actualization*.

Self-actualization means self-fulfillment, which can only be achieved by realizing our full potential, by making a contribution to the greater good, by making a difference. As you might imagine, this is the most individual of all needs and can be the most powerful. It is an internal desire to someday look back and feel as if the world, or a small piece of it, or somebody else's life, is better because of you. This craving was eloquently described by writer Leo Rosten:

"I think the purpose of life is to be useful,
to be responsible,
to be compassionate.
It is, above all, to matter:
to count,

to stand for something,
to have made some difference that you lived at all."

It is important to understand that *your* needs are different than anybody else's, so the things that motivate someone else will not necessarily inspire you, and vice versa. And your needs will change from time to time, as you mature, as your financial situation changes, as your interests change.

Following the methods in this book can help you fulfill your most important needs, whatever they are. Furthermore, it can help you get what you *want*, even if you aren't convinced that you really *need* it. Because, you see, it really doesn't matter; there doesn't have to be a conflict between needs and wants.

The dictionary defines *need* as: "Something required or wanted;…", and *want* as: "To have need of; require." They sound the same, don't they? And why shouldn't they? After all, if you want something badly enough it can become a need, can't it? And vice versa.

But it really doesn't matter whether you call it a need or a want; if you have a dream, or anything you want badly, why bother about arguing whether or not you should have it? Why should you have to convince yourself that you *need* it? Isn't the fact that you *want* it enough? Of course it is, so give yourself permission to go get it, and let me show you how.

Attitude

Although our *own* needs are important to us, they aren't the *only* needs we should think about. It's also important to understand the needs of people who are important to us, including our families, friends, and those with whom we work closely. Why? Because understanding the needs of others can make us more effective in our interpersonal relationships, which just as important in our personal lives as they are to our careers.

In fact, research has shown that there is a direct connection between employee satisfaction and customer satisfaction, and between customer satisfaction and the success of every organization. In other words, the more satisfied a company's employees are the better they will satisfy customers, and the more satisfied the customers are, the more successful the firm will be.

Translating this to a more personal level, your own level of satisfaction will have a lot to do with your attitude and enthusiasm which, in turn, affect how you come across to others. When those others are people who can affect your future success, your attitude will directly affect the impression they have of you - how *satisfied* they are with you - and can ultimately have a direct bearing on *your* success.

Where does personal satisfaction come from? Largely from how we feel about ourselves. Do we feel good about who we are; how we're doing; *what* we're doing? Or do we feel frustrated, dissatisfied, discontent, unsuccessful? When we feel good about ourselves it shows, in our attitude, our enthusiasm, the quality of our lives, and in how we come across to others.

So you see, personal satisfaction can be either a big advantage, or a major disadvantage in our relationships with others. After all, isn't it more enjoyable being around someone who is positive and upbeat, than someone who feels downtrodden and demoralized?

That's why your attitude - how you feel about yourself - can be such a powerful influence on how successful you are in realizing your dreams, achieving your goals. When you feel you're making progress, it motivates you to do whatever it takes to keep going, but when you feel as though you're a long way away from your dreams, it's discouraging, demotivating; and can make you start thinking, "I'll never get there, so why try?"

In short, your dreams and desires can be your most powerful incentives *when you believe you can achieve them,* and you'll believe they're achievable when you have a plan for reaching them. But if you can't see how to get there—if you don't have any hope at all—it can be so discouraging it affects your entire outlook on life.

Summary

The expectations we have for ourselves can have a major impact on what we do with our lives, and what we accomplish. Unfortunately, some people have themselves stereotyped; they view themselves in a certain way - who they are, and what they can and cannot do - which is often based on a fallacy, sometimes going back to childhood. And though there may be no factual evidence to support the stereotype, it can become ingrained in one's personality.

If Not Now, When?

If, for example, a teacher had once mentioned that we weren't very good at math, we might, from that point on, excuse any difficulty, such as a low math score, with "after all, I'm not very good at math." And that can easily become a self-fulfilling prophecy: the more we remind ourselves, the more we, and those around us, believe it.

And even if that teacher's observation was wrong, we may might still go through life believing we aren't very good in math, though it isn't true.

Dozens of studies have shown that students do better when their teachers have high expectations for them. The same applies to coaches - the higher their expectations for their athletes, the better those athletes perform - and managers of people - the higher their expectations for their workers, the better those workers perform.

A case in point is Clara Barton, whose heroic exploits on Civil War battlefields made her a nursing legend, and a national heroine. After the war, she continued her humanitarian efforts, both in the United States and Europe, and became the founder of the American Red Cross. Though often portrayed as an individualist and a loner, Miss Barton's deep understanding of human nature made her unusually sensitive to the needs of other people, as shown by the following example.

At one point in her career, Clara was responsible for overseeing the work of 300 women who were being paid for sewing clothing. Working independently in their homes, every few days they brought their work in to be inspected, after which they were paid.

One of Clara's assistants had been trying to help a woman whose work had been of very poor quality, but finally concluded that the woman was hopeless - her work would never be acceptable. So she took the woman to Clara, along with a skirt she had just completed. The assistant felt that the woman would have to be fired, but needed Clara to verify her opinion.

Clara quickly confirmed that the workmanship on the skirt was, indeed, very poor - totally unacceptable, in fact – but rather than condemn the woman, she inspected the skirt very carefully - every single stitch - and, after several minutes, pointed out three stitches that the woman had done exactly right; just three out of hundreds of stitches in the skirt.

Clara told the woman that, based on those three stitches, it was apparent that she was capable of sewing very well, then assured her that if she would make every stitch just like those three, her work would be among the very best of all the seamstresses.

Grateful that she had not been fired, the lady promised to do better, and returned several days later to proudly present Miss Barton with two new skirts. After careful inspection, Clara was delighted to see that every stitch was as good as the three stitches she had pointed out on the earlier skirt. Both of the new skirts were of the highest possible quality.

What made the difference? While her assistant focused on what the woman had done *wrong*, reinforcing the worker's low expectations for herself,

If Not Now, When?

Clara Barton focused on what the woman had done *right*, then emphasized Clara's high expectations for her. That apparently raised the woman's expectations for *herself*; she began to believe that she could do high quality work, and she did.

How does this apply to you? It really doesn't matter what somebody else thinks about you; it's what *you* think that counts. More importantly, it doesn't matter what somebody else thinks you *can't do*; what's really important is what *you* think you *can do*.

So why not give yourself one of the most powerful of all motivations: high expectations for yourself, and a personal plan for achieving those expectations?

Now that you know that you *should* do it, that you *can* do it, and what you'll *gain* by doing it, all you need to know is *how* to do it, which may be all that you need to reaffirm your conviction that you really *can*. But even if you're still a bit in doubt, come along with me to the next chapter and let me show you *how* to make your dream come true.

PART II

PLANNING

The purpose of planning is to decide, in advance, how to best use your knowledge, talent, money, time, and energy to achieve the goals that are most important to you. Without planning, you are likely to waste those resources reacting to whatever happens *to* you; leaving your future to the whims of fate, rather than determining your own destiny.

The chapters in this section describe the steps you should follow to develop a *personal plan* to succeed, at whatever you choose to do.

CHAPTER 4 - YOUR <u>DREAM</u>

"Cherish your visions and your dreams
as they are the children of your soul;
the blueprints of your ultimate achievements."
(Napoleon Hill, 1883-1970)

As one who has learned from experience that dreams *can* come true, I can assure you they don't come true just by dreaming. Just wishing or hoping isn't enough; you have to *make* your dreams come true.

And I'm convinced there are just two things that separate those who achieve their dreams from those who don't: 1) a clear *vision*; and 2) the *persistence* to follow that vision their dream is a reality.

Vision

Although a vision and a dream are similar, a dream is more like a wish—something you hope for—while a vision is a clear view of what you have to *do* to make your dream a reality.

Following a vision can give meaning and direction to your life, your job, your day-to-day activities, to everything you do. It clarifies where you want to go—the direction you intend to travel—and what you intend to accomplish by going that direction. Your vision is the highway to your dream. But a vision is more than that.

Your vision gives you a sense of purpose, and a plan to follow. With a vision, you're creating your own future. If you don't have a vision—a clear idea of what you're working toward, and why—you're letting your future be determined someone, or something else: by circumstances beyond your control; by whatever *happens* to you, instead of by what *you* make happen.

A vision helps focus your attention and efforts, to make sure that everything you do is somehow leading to your dream. It tells you which way to go; which hill to climb. But reaching your dream takes more than just vision; you must also have *persistence.*

Persistence

Persistence is the determination to make your dream a reality; the stamina to make it up the hill regardless of the obstacles you encounter. Persistence is the dedication that will make your dream a reality, no matter what it takes or how long. Without persistence, your dream will never come true; it will always be just a wish.

An important part of persistence is *self-direction:* the ability and willingness to take charge of yourself and your future, and that's something *anyone* can do. Self-direction is simply taking responsibility for your life; for planning who you want to be and what you want to accomplish, rather than letting circumstances, or somebody else, make those decisions for you.

If you're willing to do whatever it takes to reach your dream, and have the persistence to keep working toward it, no matter what gets in the way, you can accomplish just about anything that you set your mind to.

Summary

Vision and *persistence* are your keys to success; the two things that are absolutely essential to getting what you *want*, what you *deserve*, and what you *believe* you can have. Vision shows you the path to your dream—how you'll get there, and persistence gives you the energy and momentum to carry you all the way.

Your dream is like a beacon—a constant reminder of where you want to go, what you want to achieve. Without one you might wander aimlessly through life, responding to the crisis-of-the-moment, following the path of least resistance, or following someone else's dream, and wasting a lot of time and effort in the process.

The reward for following your dream is achieving the things that mean the most to you: your wishes, your hopes, your fondest desires.

Persistence can mold your determination and self-discipline into a force so powerful you accomplish anything you are able to envision. Benjamin Franklin's program for self improvement is a great example.

Determined to establish himself as a leader in his community, young Franklin decided he needed to re-make himself into the kind of person that others could respect, so he developed a list of thirteen virtues, and kept a daily log of how faithfully he followed them:

- Temperance - moderation in food & drink
- Silence - mentioning only important matters

- Order - proper organization of time and space
- Resolution - accomplishing one's responsibilities
- Frugality - purchasing only worthwhile items and wasting nothing
- Industry - making the most of one's time and energy
- Sincerity - being honest and forthright
- Justice - practicing impartiality and refusing to wrong others
- Moderation - avoiding extremes
- Cleanliness - using good hygiene under sanitary conditions
- Tranquility - remaining calm and composed despite life's obstacles
- Chastity - refusing to allow sex to interfere with one's life
- Humility - avoiding excess pride and haughtiness

What Ben Franklin accomplished during his lifetime is a testament to the power of determination, persistence, and self-discipline.

Once you have a clear vision for making your dream come true, and you're determined to follow it no matter what it takes, you're ready to take the first step on that path: setting goals, the subject of the next chapter.

CHAPTER 5 - SETTING GOALS

"The grand essentials to happiness in this life are
something to do,
something to love,
and something to hope for."
(Joseph Addison, 1672-1719)

Setting goals is the single most important thing you can do to get what you want.

Goals are the way you follow your vision, and the way you keep track of how you're doing.

Your dream is a destination, your *someday*; your vision is the road to that dream; and your goals are the way you travel that road, one milestone at a time.

A goal is simply a personal commitment to *do* something; to get something accomplished. Goals help focus your efforts and activities on what's most important to you; they help you work toward something specific.

People who don't set goals are more likely to waste their time and energy doing the things that are easiest or most enjoyable, while avoiding those that may be much more important. Or they work on bits and pieces of several projects, getting *something* done on each, but never *finishing* anything.

But those who set goals know that focusing their efforts and attention will someday make their dreams come true.

Which Goals?

The best way to set goals is to list everything you think needs to be done to follow your vision, to reach your dream. Goals should be vision-driven: the purpose of every goal should be to follow your vision; to move it forward.

Next, *prioritize* your list; rank your goals so you'll know which need to be done first. We never have enough time and energy to do *everything* we'd like; we always have too much to do and too little time; and most of us can only *do* one thing at a time, especially if we intend to do our *best*.

When we multi-task, we're really just shifting back and forth between one task and another, but doing it so quickly we don't have time to focus on either task for more than an instant. We may be keeping two projects going, but we're only *concentrating* on one at a time.

And remember, success is *not* measured by how many projects we keep going, but by what we accomplish: what we get *done*, and done *right*.

That's why prioritizing is so important: it helps make the best use of your time, by helping you work on the *right things*, instead of on several things. It helps you concentrate on one thing at a time—the most *important* thing—until it's complete, and done *right*, before moving on to what's next on your list.

How Many Goals?

Once you've prioritized your goals, you'll need to shorten your list, to the 4 or 5 that are most important. Having a limited number of goals is critical, because

If Not Now, When?

the fewer you set, the more likely you are to reach them.

In the extreme, if you set only *one* goal you are almost certain to reach it, because it will be the focus of all of your attention, time, and effort. It's easier to get something done when it's the only thing you have to think about.

On the other hand, the more goals you try to work on at the same time, the less your chance of completing *any* of them. So, the fewer the better, and one-at-a-time is best. That means that self-discipline is absolutely essential to reaching your goals.

It isn't easy to stay with priorities. We often have more than one person or project demanding our time, and our sense of responsibility makes us want to respond to everyone's expectations – so we don't disappoint anybody. That's certainly true for me, although I know that pleasing everyone is seldom, if ever, possible

Nevertheless, whenever I have more than one important project competing for my time (which is most of the time) I have to keep fighting the tendency to jump back and forth among them, so I won't feel guilty about not working on *all* of them, and so I can honestly reassure everyone that I am, in fact, working on their projects.

But I know that isn't a good way to work, because every time we set aside one project to work on another we lose momentum on the set-aside project, and when we come back to it we'll have to spend extra time getting back up to speed. And the more often we shift

Don O'Neal

back and forth, the more "startup" time we waste. That's why I knew I had to find a way to keep myself on track, to reduce the pressure I put on myself, and to keep me focused on doing the most important things first.

So now I schedule my time for at least a week in advance, in four-hour blocks. At least, I *try* to make each block at least 4 hours long - longer if possible - but never less than one hour. My "schedule" is an ordinary sheet of 8 ½ x 11 ruled paper, on which each space between two lines represents a day.

For example, the space between the 1st and 2nd lines represents Monday, the space between the 2nd and 3rd lines Tuesday, and so on. I mark the left edge of the sheet as 6:00 AM and the right edge as 10:00 PM, so there's room on each line to block out an entire workday.

The fact that my days run from 6 AM to 10 PM doesn't mean they're all 16 hour workdays, of course, but I do begin work at 6 quite often, and sometimes don't quit until 10, or later. But that's me. The important thing is that your hours are those that best fit *your* preferred schedule.

The first blocks I schedule are for my ongoing commitments (e.g., class times, committee meetings,) which reserves those times so I won't inadvertently schedule them for something else.

Then I pencil in the other projects I intend to work on during that week, choosing them by priorities and deadlines, to make sure I can clearly see that the time necessary for completing each of my major commitments is somewhere on the schedule. (For major projects, I sometimes have to schedule several weeks in advance, so I can visualize their completion dates.)

Since writing is a top priority for me, I try to set aside the first few hours of every morning for it. Of course I occasionally have to work in other things (e.g., doctor's appointments,) but I try to schedule them when they'll interfere the least.

This system solves the "pressure" problems that I described earlier. I can work on one thing at a time without feeling guilty about neglecting the other projects, because I know they're on the schedule, and I know when they're scheduled to be completed. This allows me to reassure everyone that their projects will get done on time, even though I may not be working on them at the moment, and I can even give them estimated completion dates.

It's amazing how much this system has reduced the pressure, both external and self-imposed, and how much peace of mind it gives me, because I know it will all get done, that I'll do it in a way that gets the results I want and, best of all, I know I'm making good use of my time and energy.

This method not only increases the amount of work I get done but also the quality. It may sound complicated, but all it takes to create this type of schedule, including revising it when necessary, is a single sheet of paper and no more that 15 minutes each week. And the best part is that I'm not working any harder, but I'm getting a lot more accomplished, with a lot less stress. When you try it, you'll see what I mean.

Measurable Goals

Now that you have a shortened, prioritized list, you'll need to describe each goal in a way that will allow you to measure it, so you'll always know how you're doing; how well you're moving toward it.

For a goal to be *measurable*, it must be stated in such a way that it answers three questions:

1. How *much?*
2. Of *what?*
3. By *when?*

Always begin with Question 2, Of *what?* which refers to the goal, itself - *what* is it that you intend to accomplish? what is your desired result?
(e.g., completion of the first set of required courses for your degree in Journalism; a home-made cake; completed endurance races.)

Then Question 1, How *much?* which asks you the desired *amount* (i.e., quantity) of that goal?
(e.g., 3 courses; 1 cake; 2 marathons)

And, finally, Question 3, By *when?* which asks for a deadline—*when* do you plan to have this goal completed?
(e.g., by the end of next semester; by tomorrow morning; by the end of the year)

Now you have examples of measurable goals: completing the first three required courses toward a degree in Journalism by the end of the next semester; baking a cake by tomorrow morning; and completing two marathons by the end of the year. Each goal says *what* you're going to do, *how much* of it, and by *when*.

Any goal that isn't stated that way, in terms that answer all three questions, is *not* measurable, and any goal that isn't measurable is *useless,* because it isn't a *commitment;* it's only a vague wish. When you have measurable goals you'll not only know *when* you've reached a goal, you can measure your progress along the way. Why is it so important for goals to be measurable?

Because following a long-term plan isn't always a straightforward process. There will be times when things seem to be moving so slowly it's hard to see any progress at all, and other times when things are happening so fast the process may seem to be out of control.

When things are moving slowly, comparing today's measurements with those from last week, or last month, or even last year can reassure you that you *are* making progress. And when things appear to be happening too fast, comparing where you are today with where you had *planned* to be at this time can either convince you that things are *not* out of control, or allow you to slow things down if they *are* going too fast.

That's why it is so important for your goals to be measurable—they give you a way of evaluating how you're doing at any stage of the process.

Tradeoffs

Every time you set a goal, you're making a decision about how to invest your time and energy. Since we all have limited supplies of both, it's important to utilize them in the most effective manner, to achieve the best possible results for our time and effort.

Since we're all different, our dreams will be different, our visions will be different, our goals will be different, and the choices we make will be different, too.

The hardest part of choosing is that getting what we want nearly always requires giving up something else. Making choices would be easy if we could have anything we need or want, but that's hardly ever the case. Most of us will never have all of the *money* we would like, nor an unlimited supply of *energy*. And *time*, of course, is the most scarce of all resources; we are allotted only a certain amount of it-24 hours a day, and nobody knows how many days.

So, because we can't *do* everything we'd like to do, and we can't *have* everything we'd like to have, we have to make choices, and we have to *give up* things. For everything we choose to do or have, there will be something else that we *can't* do, or *can't* have.

Those kinds of tradeoffs can play a major role in your success; how you choose to invest your time and energy; what you're willing to give up in exchange for making your dreams come true. So deciding what you *can't* do, or *won't* do, becomes just as important as deciding what you *will* do.

Summary

Never underestimate the power of goals. It's amazing what we can accomplish when we convince ourselves that a particular thing not only *can* be done but *will* be done, then direct the full force of our efforts to making sure it *does* get done.

You should always consider your goals to be dynamic, not static, because goals tend to be moving targets. Although your initial plan will be to pursue each goal until you've reached it, now and then you'll have to change one *before* you reach it. So you'll need to keep a close eye on your goals, to make sure you see when circumstances change, and you can determine whether or not your plan needs to change accordingly.

Then every time you achieve a goal, make it a point to start on the *next* one right away. Goals, themselves, are simply *means* to an end: to your dream. They are milemarkers on the road of your vision; the way you measure your progress.

Although your vision isn't likely to change, at least until you've reached your dream, your goals may have to evolve throughout the process.

CHAPTER 6 – WHAT YOU'LL **DO**

"You will never find time for anything.
If you want time you must make it."
(Robert Burton 1577-1640)

Once you've set goals – exactly what you need to get done – it's time to decide exactly how you'll go about achieving them: what actions you'll have to take, and in what order.

Organizing your activities into an action plan is a three-step process: 1) listing your actions and activities – what you're going to do to achieve each goal; 2) scheduling those actions and estimating the time it will take to complete each one, along with the dates you intend to start and finish them; then 3) determining what resources you'll need, when you'll need them, and how you intend to get them.

Actions

You should begin by listing *everything* that needs to be done - every activity, task, or action - to reach your most important goal. Then do the same for the rest of your goals (the other 3 or 4,) so you can see if there are any activities that overlap, affect other activities, or serve more than one goal. Usually it takes several actions (e.g., activities, tasks) to reach a single goal, so your final list may be fairly long.

If Not Now, When?

Schedule

Next, schedule your activities in the order they need to be done. While there are usually some activities that can be done any time, and in any order, there are likely to be some that can't be done until others have been completed. So you'll need to schedule your activities in the order that will get them done in the right sequence and in the shortest amount of time.

College students, for example, know there are some courses they're not allowed to take until after others - called prerequisites - have been completed, so they arrange their schedules to take the prerequisites first, then schedule the other courses in the appropriate order.

Once you have what looks like a workable schedule - a sequence of activities that seems to make sense - you can estimate the *timing* of your activities: how long it will take to complete each one, in terms of *work hours,* or *work days*. You should also schedule the *dates* on which you plan to begin and complete each activity. These not only provides milestones, to help you measure how you're doing at any time, but also add a sense of urgency to your plan, as well as a "light at the end of the tunnel."

Once you've worked out times and dates, your schedule will serve as a calendar of your future activities for some period of time, but remember, at this point it's only a preliminary plan; you still need to determine what resources you'll need, when you'll need them, and how you'll get them.

Resources

Resources, of course, include everything you'll need for each activity – information, knowledge, skills, equipment, time, money, etc.

The idea is to make sure you have the resources you need for each activity *before* you actually need them. That way, if it looks as though getting a resource may be a problem, you can either find alternate sources, or revise your schedule to reflect when the resource *will* be available. The value of planning resource-availability ahead of time is illustrated by the following example.

Suppose one of your activities requires knowledge or skills that you don't currently have, and the date you have scheduled to begin that activity is only three months away – not enough time for you to learn that skill (e.g., a new software program). There are two ways you can solve this problem: hire someone who has those skills, or reschedule that activity to a later date so you'll have time to learn the skills, yourself. The first option depends on being able to find and hire the right person, in the time available, at a price you can afford. The other choice may be less expensive but it, too, has a cost: delaying your schedule.

Although this type of dilemma is sometimes unavoidable, scheduling your activities far enough in advance that you have options - back-up plans for what you will do when something doesn't go as planned - can help make sure that you reach your goals, effectively and on time.

Control

In the final analysis, perhaps the most important ingredient in getting, and keeping, yourself on schedule is *self-discipline:* the determination to make sure *you're* the one who controls what you do and when you do it, rather than letting yourself be controlled by someone or something else. Once you've set your schedule you should do everything you can to stick to it, and not allow yourself to be easily distracted, by anyone or anything. The key word is *easily*.

There will inevitably be times when something appears to be more important than your schedule, but when that happens just make sure it really *is* more important before you let it interrupt your schedule. Don't let yourself be interrupted just because you hate to say "No". It's always tempting to give in to requests like "this will only take a couple of minutes" or "just let me interrupt you for a minute", but when you give in to one it is likely to be followed by another, and another, until finally another day is gone and you haven't accomplished what you had planned, and you realize you're falling farther and farther behind schedule. This happens much too often; perhaps it has happened to you; it certainly has to me.

I have always started my day with a list, actually a *prioritized* list, of the things I intended to do that day. But it didn't always work out as I had planned; in fact it seldom did. Many times I'd work hard all day, sometimes even staying late, yet leave work with *nothing* crossed off my list. But that's not a problem for me any more (at least not as often,) because I've developed a system for keeping myself on track.

First, I learned to say "no" to the things that weren't really important. I say it in a nice way, but firmly, and without feeling as though I have to give a reason, or any explanation at all. Of course, when the person making the request is my boss, or my wife, I am less likely to say "no," or more likely to give a reason if I do. To make my system work, I came up with a method for deciding what was really important and what wasn't, based on four rules of thumb: one for mail; one for phone calls; one for paperwork; and one for "walk-ins."

When I go through my mail (both at my office and at home) anything that doesn't come with first-class postage gets thrown out, with rare exceptions. Most of the time if it isn't first class, it's just someone trying to sell something, and why should I waste my time reading junk mail?

Thanks to "Caller ID", I no longer answer phone calls that don't have identifying phone numbers (for example, those labeled "out of area"). Why should I waste time listening to an unsolicited invasion of my time and privacy?

I treat work-related paperwork just like mail, although the way I do it isn't quite as final as throwing it out. I put any document that isn't *obviously* important - important enough to interrupt me right now – into a *three-day* file. Then, every day I take a few minutes to look at the file from the bottom up - everything that's been in there for three days - to see if there's anything that looks more urgent than when I put

If Not Now, When?

it in. You'd be amazed at how much of what's in there has solved itself, or has been taken care of by somebody else, during those three days. And when something in the file turns out to be more important than I had originally thought, someone is sure to let me know about it, so I can reconsider it. But that doesn't happen very often, which suggests that a lot of the paperwork we handle isn't so important that three days will make a difference. In fact, as it turns out, a lot of the paperwork we receive isn't very important at all.

Finally, the "walk-ins" - people who see that I'm in the office, and drop in for a chat. When this happens, I simply *stand up* as they enter, then quickly determine if what they have to discuss is important or not. If it is, and it appears that it will take some time to discuss, I invite them to sit down. But when it isn't important, I remain standing, and they usually won't sit down unless I do, and seldom stay longer than a minute or two unless I encourage further discussion. It works like a charm, almost every time. And when it does, *I* control when I can be interrupted and when I can't.

Summary

Making sure you reach your goals, *when* you intend to, requires an action plan, including: a list of the actions to be taken, a schedule of dates and times, and a list of the resources you'll need.

Your plan should start with a *list* of everything that has to happen to reach your goals; a list will make you fully aware of the size and scope of the task.

Next you *schedule* those actions/activities, to make sure that you do them in the necessary order, with special attention to those activities that have to be done before others can be started.

Then comes *timing*: determining how much time and effort will be required for each activity, and setting times and dates for beginning and completing them.

Finally, you determine what *resources* you'll need to reach your goals, and see if there are any conflicts in the *availability* of resources that might make rescheduling necessary.

And perhaps the most important thing to remember is that, once your schedule is finalized, you must have enough *self-discipline* to avoid being sidetracked by anyone or anything that isn't as important as your goals.

CHAPTER 7 - HOW YOU'LL <u>SUCCEED</u>

"In idle wishes fools supinely stay;
be there a will, and wisdom finds a way."
(George Crabbe, 1754-1832)

Now that you've set goals, and have an action plan for reaching them, you need just one more thing: a commitment to make it all happen.

In Chapter 4, I said "Persistence is the dedication that will make you dream a reality, no matter what it takes or how long." Remember?

Well now it's time to make that kind of commitment, to yourself and to your dream, the kind of commitment that comes from a combination of *initiative*, *persistence*, and *focus*.

Initiative

Initiative simply means doing things on your own, without having to be told. Initiative is part of self-direction; taking responsibility for your own actions; not having to wait for orders. It's the difference between people who are self-starters and those who only take action when pushed by someone else.

Initiative isn't some mysterious talent that some people have and others don't; everyone has it, but not everyone uses it. If you want to follow *your* vision, to *your* dream, instead of following someone else's, you'll have to take initiative, because if you wait for someone else to spur you into action, it may never happen; you may never do it.

So you're going to need that initiative *now*, even if it's a bit rusty; or if you've never used it before. Why? Because now you're going to do something that *you want to do*, not what someone else wants you to do. This is *your* dream, *your* passion, and you're going to do whatever it takes to make it come true. And it will take initiative to get you started.

You've taken the time and effort to put together a good, solid plan, now it's time to put it into action, and that's where initiative is so important; it's the difference between a dream that comes true, and one that never happens. Although lots of people develop wonderful plans, most of them remain just plans, dreams, hopes. Why?

Because a plan can't put itself into action; it takes a person to do that, and a lot of people just don't have the initiative to take that first step toward converting their plans into action. But that won't be you. You've waited long enough for this dream, and you won't have to wait any longer.

The first step is the hardest, because you have to overcome inertia (our natural resistance to change), perhaps years of inertia. Take me, for example.

As I write this, I am a full-time professor, with responsibilities that keep me busy more than 40 hours a week. But I need to write; it's important to me; I have thoughts, experience and information I want to share, and I have to find a way to do it; a way to work it in around my "real" job.

So I do my writing early in the morning, which means getting up while most other people are still snug and warm in bed. Believe me, getting out of bed at 5:00 in the morning takes initiative, and it takes it *every day*, not just once in a while. What gives me the initiative?

I love to write, and I relish the thought that my writing may help other people. For me, that's exciting! Writing is my dream, and it's worth getting up early for. If it weren't, I couldn't do it; I *wouldn't* do it.

So if you're as passionate about your dream as I am about mine, initiative won't be a problem for you, either. And once you feel the satisfaction of the results you'll get (for me, that's a book, or a published paper), your initiative will feed on itself, and you won't have to drive yourself so hard; your sense of accomplishment will do that for you.

Persistence

But initiative by itself isn't enough. It's one thing to get started, but keeping going is something else again. Staying with your vision until you realize your dream takes persistence: the determination to follow through no matter what you have to do, or overcome, in the process. You must have determination, because the road to your dream won't always be smooth, it won't always be straight, it won't always be downhill, and you can be sure there will sometimes be obstacles and detours. Let's use you as an example.

Suppose you've always dreamed of visiting the Grand Canyon, and now (inspired by this book) you've

Don O'Neal

finally decided to do it. After considering all of the things we've discussed so far (i.e., vision, goals, etc.), you have a plan to drive from your home, in Chicago, to the Grand Canyon, (more than 1000 miles,) and seeing some sights along the way.

It calls for overnight stops in Oklahoma City (1st night) Albuquerque, New Mexico (2nd night), Flagstaff, Arizona (3rd night), and the Grand Canyon (4th and 5th nights), then a return trip which includes several sightseeing side-trips over a five-day period. You plan to leave early (6:00 AM) on Friday, July 17th, and arrive back home on Sunday, July 27th. You've planned the trip in detail, including hotel reservations for the first 5 nights.

The evening before you leave, you gas up the car and load up all of your family's luggage, so all you'll have to do the next morning is get up, get dressed, and take off.

But, as sometimes happens, the next morning doesn't go exactly as planned, and you don't get on the road until 7:00, an hour later than planned. But you tell yourself that's not a major problem; you may be able to make up some of that time during the day but, if not, you'll just get to your motel later than you had planned. Your breakfast stop comes off without a hitch and you're on the road again but, as you get close to St. Louis, traffic comes to a complete stop.

At first you assume it's either construction or an accident, and that the tie-up will be relatively short, but an hour later you get word that a bridge over the

If Not Now, When?

Mississippi River has been damaged by a runaway barge, and traffic is being re-routed.

By the time you're on your way again, several hours later, you realize you'll never make it to Oklahoma City tonight, so you make the necessary phone calls to cancel those reservations and make reservations somewhere else. So you've missed your first goal, but that doesn't mean the end of your dream; just a temporary setback. You didn't get quite as far as you'd planned the first day, so you'll have to figure out how it will affect the rest of your plan.

Of course you have lots of options: you can drive further tomorrow and make it to where you had originally planned to stay the second night; you can cut out a planned visit to Amarillo; or you can change where you had intended to stay the second and third nights. Sounds a bit frustrating, doesn't it? Of course, and it sometimes *is* frustrating; that's why determination is so important: it overcomes frustration; keeps it in perspective.

It's easy to get where you're going when everything goes according to plan, but everything doesn't always go as planned, and that's when some people give up and turn back.

But others - those with persistence - keep going; they work around the obstacles; they find a way. They won't give up on their dream no matter what happens. That's persistence, and that's what it takes to get where you want to go. There will always be obstacles and detours, but determination will always find a way. In the worst of conditions you may even have to abandon your quest, but when you persist, most setbacks will only be temporary; not permanent.

For example, I see lots of mature students who come back to complete their education after being out of school for years. For one reason or another, they had to give up their dream for a while, but they didn't give it up completely. Their plans were delayed, but they were persistent; they came back.

Focus

Focus is what helps you keep your eye on the target, and not let anything else distract you. Focus is about concentrating on your vision. With so many things competing for our attention every day, it's hard to concentrate on just one. But that's what you'll have to do.

You have to determine what's most important to you and focus on that, and pretty much ignore everything else. Of course, it's understood that some things may be more important than your vision - your family, and your job, for instance - but anything that isn't more important shouldn't be allowed to distract you.

Focus is essential, not only to keep you from wasting time on unimportant things, but also to help you concentrate. I don't have to tell you how frustrating it is to be in the middle of something and get interrupted, then try to get back to where you were before the interruption. Whether you're reading, writing, or just thinking, interruptions break your train of thought; they break your concentration; and it may be difficult, if not impossible, to recapture exactly the thought that was interrupted. For that reason, I've developed a system that makes it easier for me to stay focused.

I set aside certain times when I don't allow interruptions. When I'm writing, that time is always in the morning. Although it's impossible to avoid *all* interruptions, I make sure that when I allow myself to be interrupted it's for a darned good reason, and it's at my discretion. I don't let anyone else plan my mornings for me. I try to make every morning *mine*, and I guard them jealously.

That ensures that I have several hours of uninterrupted time every morning - time to concentrate – which makes mornings my most productive time. I'd suggest that you do something similar.

Set aside certain times, on a regular schedule, that you consider inviolable; times that you won't allow anybody to infringe upon. For me, it's the early part of the day, but for you it may be late at night, after everyone else is in bed, maybe your lunch hour, or Saturday mornings, or Sunday afternoons.

If you're anything like me, you don't have a lot of spare time, so you're going to have to *take* time, or *make* time, to follow your dream. Because without focus - without the ability to concentrate on what you're doing - you'll never get there.

Summary

Your plan is an important milestone; it's your formula for turning your dream into a reality. But the plan itself won't help you at all unless you put it into action. It's up to you to make it happen, and that takes commitment: the willingness to overcome every obstacle, and see your plan through to its successful conclusion.

Perhaps the hardest part of executing any plan is getting started; taking the first step. That takes *initiative*. Once you've done that and have it moving, it's essential to *keep* it moving; to not lose your momentum in spite of any obstacles you may encounter. That takes *persistence*. And while it's rolling you have to keep it on course; don't lose sight of where you're going; don't get sidetracked. That takes *focus*.

Those three elements - initiative, persistence, and focus - will help you keep your commitments, and that's the biggest difference between those who make their dreams come true and those who just dream and hope.

So make up your mind, right now, that nothing will keep you from getting started, or from moving forward, or from focusing your time, efforts and attention on doing whatever is necessary to make your dream a reality.

PART III

DOING

Now that you have a plan, you have to do something with it: put it into action; start making your vision a reality. This is often the most difficult part of having a plan, because so many things can get in the way of anything we try to do. So our purpose in this section is to make sure your plan doesn't remain just a plan; that you *do* what you've planned.

The chapters in this section show you how to make your plan happen the way you planned it, by *organizing* your time and activities, assessing the *external environment*, *evaluating* your *progress*, and *managing change.*

CHAPTER 8 - AIMING HIGH

"Hold yourself responsible for a higher standard
than anyone else expects of you."
(Henry Ward Beecher, 1813-1887)

Expectations

When he learned that I had accepted a job with a large company, a friend remarked, "That company has thousands of employees; aren't you afraid you'll be just a *number*?" Since this was my first "real" job after college - all of my work experience had been in summer jobs, working for individuals and small businesses - I didn't have an answer for his question.

But experience taught me that, although what he said is often true – that many people in large organizations *do* feel like they're just numbers - it doesn't *have* to be that way. It didn't take me long to learn that the way you feel about yourself, in any organization, depends on *you*; that it *is* possible to stand out, even in a big company, if you set high expectations for yourself.

Although that may not sound like an earth-shaking discovery, it turned out to be one of the most valuable lessons I've ever learned, and has had an enormous influence on my career, so it bears repeating:

Aiming high, by setting high expectations for yourself can be one of the most powerful tools you'll ever find to help you in your life, your career, and in reaching your dreams.

When people work in organizations, they usually set their expectations according to the people they work with; they try to do their jobs in ways that ensure that they'll keep pace with everyone else. In fact, in some work environments there's an unwritten understanding that nobody works *too* hard, lest they make others look bad by comparison, and anyone who violates it is likely to be cautioned, "Slow down. What are you trying to do, increase our production rate?"

As a result, in most organizations the work gets done at the most comfortable pace that's acceptable to management, where "acceptable" means the *minimum* acceptable amount of work.

And when you work in that kind of environment you have a choice: become one of the many who are content to do average work, or one of the few who aren't willing to settle for anything less than their best.

While it may be easier, or more comfortable, being one of the faceless multitude – just a number – that *isn't* the road to personal success. Pride, satisfaction, and success come from setting high standards for yourself; trying to be better than just "good enough." The choice is yours, but you should be aware that choosing to excel won't always be an easy path, because it isn't likely to make you popular with everyone, especially those who think you're making *them* look bad.

Let's say, for example, that you've become an outstanding performer at work (by applying the principles of this book, of course.) You'll be happy about that, your boss will be happy about it, your family will be happy about it, everyone will be happy, right? Unfortunately, no; not *everyone* will be happy.

Some of your co-workers, those whose performance is good, but not outstanding, may *not* enjoy your good fortune. They may feel that your high level of performance is making them look bad by comparison. Although you're meeting your *own* expectations, you're *not* meeting *theirs*, which are probably something like "maintain the status quo," or "don't rock the boat." In other words, they'd like it better if your performance was more like theirs; if it was just *good*; if it was *average*. So now you have them worried, and they may even start pressuring you to slow down, to "ease off," and if you don't, they may find ways to make your work-life less enjoyable, or even try to undercut you.

When this happens (and it's an unfortunate fact of organizational life that it *does* happen, more often than many people realize,) you have a choice. Give in to their concerns and slow down; anything to keep peace in the workplace, right? But if you do that, you'll be taking the easy way out; and you'll be selling out *your* dreams to make up for someone else's lack of ambition.

So when this situation comes up, you can either do what they want, or be true to yourself. Now I shouldn't have to tell you which is the right choice; you know it as well as I do. So remind yourself that it's *their* problem, not yours, and keep on doing your best.

Because if you take the easy way out, and give in to the fears of others, you'll be the loser. You'll be sacrificing yourself and your dreams, and for what?

What will you get for what you're giving up? Back in their good graces? Maybe, but will it be *worth* it?

And don't forget about the others who will also be losers if you give in: your family, for example, and your employer. So remember, the fact that you work harder or smarter than someone else won't put them at a disadvantage unless they *let* it; unless they aren't willing to work as hard as you; aren't willing to pay the same price.

Remember, you aren't trying to be better than them; you're not competing with *them*; you're competing with *yourself*; trying to be the best that *you* can be.

And when you excel, don't expect everyone to give you credit for what you accomplish. Some will find it too painful to admit that you did something better than they, and may even say it's because you're just "lucky," even if you've worked and sacrificed for *years* to accomplish what you have.

So you have to learn to ignore what those people think; you'll never be able to satisfy *everyone*, so just make sure you satisfy those who really matter, beginning with yourself. And think about when times get tough, and the company has to downsize. Who will be the first to go—the best performers, or those who are content to be average? You know the answer as well as I: most companies will do everything possible to keep their best people.

Meeting high expectations doesn't require more skills, or better skills, or more knowledge than anyone else. Exceptional performance just means giving a bit more than the average person; working a bit *harder*, being a bit more *committed* to getting the job done, and doing work that's a bit *better*. You don't have to be a genius, you just have to do *your best*, every time, and in every situation.

An interesting thing about expectations is that those we have for ourselves in the workplace are often very different than those we have when we're doing something for ourselves, *outside* the organization.

When we're doing things *we* want to do (e.g., woodworking, art, gardening, traveling,) we usually set high expectations for ourselves without even thinking about it; it's automatic. Why is it so different in the organizations where we work?

I think a lot of it has to do with *recognition*: who gets the credit when a job is done well, and who gets the blame when it isn't.

When it's our own project, we get personal satisfaction from knowing we did our best, we take pride in what we accomplish, and if we don't do it well, it hurts our pride.

Unfortunately, in companies, those who actually *do* the work don't always get the recognition they deserve, but when things *don't* go well, they often get a share of the blame.

We may not be able to change the way our companies give recognition, but we shouldn't let that affect the quality of our work. You should always be true to yourself, and make sure you don't let the company's shortcomings affect your *personal* expectations.

By that I mean you owe it to yourself, and to your self-esteem, to always do your best, even when you know it may not be recognized by others. You can take comfort in the knowledge that *you* will appreciate it and, in the final analysis, it's *your* opinion that matters.

Setting high expectations, and reaching them, benefits us in two ways: the satisfaction we get from achieving what we set out to do, and the pride that comes from knowing that we did our best.

Now you may already *be* the kind of person who works hard to satisfy yourself; constantly trying to improve on what you've done before; continually raising your expectations for yourself. But if you're *not*, I'll help you do something about it, and we'll begin by setting expectations.

There are two parts to setting expectations: *what* you expect, and *how well* you expect to do it. You've already taken the first step: deciding *what* you expect. Those are the *goals* you've set, which we talked about in Chapter 5. The second part, *how well* you do in reaching your goals will have a lot to do with your capabilities, your strengths, the things that you know how to do best.

The next chapter discusses how to analyze your capabilities, and Chapter 10 covers how you can evaluate how well you're using those your capabilities to reach your goals.

Summary

Everyone has the opportunity to excel. It begins with the determination not to settle for being average, or "good enough."

The expectations we set for ourselves become our standards of performance, and if you want yours to be above average, you have to set expectations that are higher than the average person. "Why," you might ask, "should I try for above-average performance? Why excel?"

The benefits should be self-evident. Just think about what you'll gain; what it can do for your work-life and career. And even more important is what it can do for your pride and self- esteem, and the satisfaction you'll get from doing outstanding work. You'll feel better about yourself and everything you do.

Here are some questions to guide you in setting expectations: "What are *my* expectations for myself? How well am I meeting them? How can I do better? " and "*Who else's* expectations am I trying to meet? How am I doing? How can I do better?"

You owe it to yourself to be better than just *good* at what you do; to always try to be the best that you can be. And remember:

Good Enough Isn't Good Enough

> My friend, beware of "good enough,"
> it isn't made of sterling stuff;
> it's something anyone can do;
> it marks the many from the few.

Don O'Neal

The flaw which may escape the eye
and temporarily get by,
shall weaken underneath the strain,
and wreck the ship, the car or plane.

With "good enough," the car breaks down,
and one falls short of high renown.

My friend, remember and be wise,
in "good enough," disaster lies.

With "good enough," the shirkers stop
in every factory, school, and shop;
with "good enough," the failures rest
and lose to the one who gives the best.

Who stops at "good enough" shall find
success has left them far behind.

For this is true for you and your stuff—
only the best is "good enough."

(Author unknown)

CHAPTER 9 - **LOOKING AHEAD**

"The only fence against the world
is a thorough knowledge of it."
(John Locke, 1632-1704)

Success comes from reaching our goals, but getting there is sometimes more difficult that we had planned. No matter how we try, there are times when things don't go according to plan; when something threatens to keep us from getting where we want to go; something we can't do anything about.

This happens because, although we can control *some* things, there are always others that we *can't*. The purpose of this chapter is to show you how to look at what's going on in the world around you, analyze which parts of it might affect you, and determine what you can do about them.

The Outside World

Figure 1 is a simple diagram of your relationship with the outside world.

INPUTS ⟶ | YOU | ⟶ OUTPUTS

Figure 1.

Inputs are the things you need to complete a project; to do what you want to accomplish; to reach your goal.

For example, if you want to bake a cake, you'll need the ingredients (flour, sugar, eggs, etc.,) tools (cooking utensils, and a stove,) a recipe (information – how to do it,) and the money to buy any of those inputs that you don't already have. And if any of those inputs are missing, you won't be able to bake the cake.

Outputs are your goals—in this case, a cake. They're your results, the outcomes of what you do, what you get for your efforts. If you're doing something for yourself, you can control the outputs, and the outside world may not affect you at all. But if you're doing it for someone else, you can't control how *they'll* feel about what you've done, and although *you* may be pleased with the result, *they* may *not* be. So you'll have to make sure, in advance, exactly what they expect, then plan your process to make sure you achieve that result.

That's just one example of why it's so important to understand what goes on around us. The outputs we produce depend on, first, getting the inputs we need – from the outside world - then on how our outputs are judged, usually by someone who is also in the outside world. Therefore, our success is often determined by how well we are able to deal with the uncertainties of the outside world.

Fortunately, we don't have to deal with the *entire* world; only the parts of it that might affect our inputs and outputs. But we may not be able to control even those parts, and when we can't control them it's difficult to predict how they might affect us, or when, or where.

The *You* in Figure 1 represents everything you *can* control: your knowledge, skills, and abilities, and what you do with them; how you use them.

Even though you can't always control your ability to get the inputs you need, when you need them, nor can you control how your outputs are judged by those who receive them, you *can* control the *process* of turning those inputs into outputs.

Uncertainty

When we can't control something, we can't predict how it will affect us, so we won't know whether or not it will keep us from reaching our goals. But although we can't *eliminate* uncertainty, we can sometimes *reduce* it, and make the part of the outside world that affects us a bit more predictable.

To do that, we have to know what to look for; the types of things that are most likely to affect us. If we know *what* to look, we may be able to predict what is *likely* to happen, before it happens.

Suppose, for example, I throw you a ball. As soon as you see it coming you will instinctively "predict" what you have to do to catch it, or to avoid being hit by it. At first you may not know *exactly* where it will hit, but as you watch it coming you will automatically narrow down the possible target area; and the closer it gets the better you're able to predict where it's going to hit.

So, although you can't keep me from throwing it – you can't control what *I* do - you can control how *you* respond to it, either by catching the ball or getting out of the way. We do this all the time, often without consciously thinking about it.

Another example is how, when driving a car, we predict whether or not we will have time to pass the car in front of us without colliding with oncoming cars. We do this by rapidly estimating the distance between our car and the other one, and how fast the other car is traveling, and we do it instinctively; almost without thinking about it.

We make these types of predictions by using some combination of experience, perception, attention, and reaction, and an important part of the process is observing *trends*—we see what *has* happened (the ball has been thrown), watch what *is* happening (it's coming right toward me), and estimate what *will* probably happen next (it's going to hit me)—and we respond accordingly (I'll try to catch it.)

But you can only see trends if you *look* for them, by observing what's going on in the world around you. The better you become at spotting trends, the better you'll be able to predict what's likely to happen, and be prepared for it, in a way that keeps you in control. But not many people do that, and that's the big difference between those people who always seem to know, in advance, what's going to happen, and those who are often caught off guard.

Once you've become an experienced trend-spotter, you'll be better able to see what's going on in the world around you, and better equipped to determine which trends are likely to affect you, and which you needn't worry about. And you'll be better prepared to recognize opportunities where others see only threats.

Opportunities and Threats

A *threat* can be anything that looks as though it might harm us, or make life more difficult, while an *opportunity* can be anything that looks like it might help us, or make things easier. But most of the time they're the same thing; the only difference being how we view them. What looks like a threat to one person will invariably be seen as an opportunity by someone else. What makes people view them differently?

It has a lot to do with how *surprised* we are when something happens. If we see it developing ahead of time, before it starts to affect us, we're more likely to be prepared for it, and more likely to see the opportunities it presents. But if we're caught off guard because we *didn't* see it coming, we're more likely to view the same situation as a threat.

Almost any kind of change can be seen as either a threat or an opportunity. However, as a general rule, more people see change as a *threat* than an opportunity. But why don't more people see the opportunities? And why aren't more people ready for change, *before* it starts affecting them?

Usually it has to do with how forward-looking they are; whether they keep an eye to the future, or just think about what's happening *now*.

Those who make it a point to constantly observe what's going on around them, and look for trends, are able to see the future as it develops, and to *predict* how it may affect them, and their plans. They can determine, in advance, how to prepare for what's going to happen, and look for the opportunities, not just than threats.

On the other hand, people who *don't* look ahead are much more likely to be surprised and confused by the uncertainty that comes with change, and are often so overwhelmed they let the circumstances manage *them*, instead of the other way around.

For them, any change is likely to appear threatening. Ironically, these are often the same people who declare "I don't have time to plan for the future; I'm too busy." Maybe they should ask themselves, instead, "Or am I too busy because I don't *take* time to plan?" In any case, make sure you're not one of them. Make sure you manage your future; don't let it manage you.

The first step toward managing your future - to controlling the part of the outside world that affects you - is realizing that you *can* do something about what's happening around you; that you don't have to let the outside world manage you.

Then you have to know *how* to manage the future, which is an important part of believing that you *can*. And if you know how, it's much easier to convince yourself that you *can*. So, here's the way to manage your outside world, and turn threats into opportunities.

First, recognize that it isn't possible to know *everything* that's going on in the outside world. As we discussed earlier in this chapter, all you need to be concerned with are those parts that are likely to affect you and your plan, which are only a small piece of the world. And you learn about those parts by boundary scanning.

Boundary Scanning

Boundary scanning is simply looking for anything you think might affect what you do or how you do it. One way is reading newspapers and magazines that give different perspectives on the topics you're interested in. Well-regarded daily newspapers (e.g., Wall Street Journal, New York Times, Chicago Tribune, Washington Post) are good sources, and so are magazines and trade publications that relate to your profession, your area of expertise, or your interests. They'll keep you informed about what's going on in your areas of interest.

Other ways of boundary scanning include the internet, networking with friends and business associates, and the organizations you belong to.

It doesn't matter *how* you do it, it's just important that you *do* it, because boundary scanning is your window on the world; it can provide information that will help you spot trends, and changes in trends, *before* they become threats—while they can still be opportunities.

But boundary-scanning brings with it a new dilemma: with so much information to sort through, how will you know which information is useful and which isn't? What should you look for? What should you keep? And what should you ignore?

Think back to the beginning of this chapter, and our discussion of the outside world and how it affects *inputs* and *outputs*. Your primary concern with the external world is how it affects your ability to get the inputs you need and how to control your outputs.

If you can't get the inputs you need, when you need them, you won't be able to do whatever it is you're trying to do. If you can't get the ingredients for the cake, you won't be able to bake it. And even if you can get the ingredients, but can't find anybody who wants the cake, what's the point of baking it (unless you intend to eat the whole thing yourself)? So the only parts of the external world that need your attention are those that affect your inputs and your outputs.

Inputs

Whatever you're trying to do—get a degree, remodel a house, or bake a cake—you have to make sure you can get the inputs you need when you need them.

There are many things you can do to reduce the uncertainty of obtaining inputs: keep a reserve supply (an inventory,) or buy from more than one supplier (to make sure what you need is always available, regardless of what happens to a single supplier); perform preventive maintenance (to ensure that work flow isn't interrupted by equipment failures); take training (to make sure you have the necessary knowledge and skills *when* they're needed.) Following are a few examples of strategies for making sure that you always have the inputs you need.

Where *raw material*, *equipment*, and *information* are concerned, you'll need to manage availability (what you need, when you need it) and cost (the right price). Both are affected by supply and demand. How much of what you need is available? If there's more demand than supply the cost will be higher and delivery slower, but when there's more supply than demand, the cost will be lower and delivery faster. Boundary scanning is how you monitor supply and demand, and how you know when you can buy at the lowest price, and where. You're probably already a bargain shopper, aren't you? If so, you already know how to do this.

If you don't have the *knowledge* that's required, you can get it either through education and training, or by hiring someone who already has the knowledge.

If you hire somebody else, you'll have to consider availability and cost. You'll need to look at supply and demand again, this time from a human perspective. How many people are there with the knowledge you need, what's the demand for their services, and what will it cost.

If you decide to acquire the knowledge yourself, time will be a major concern (how long will it take to get the training or education you need?) and so will availability (where and when will you be able to get the training or education that you need?)

Then there's *money*, perhaps your most important input. You'll need it to purchase your other inputs, and maybe even to support you while you follow your dream. For most of us, money comes from wages, savings, or borrowing. When it's from wages, you'll need to keep an eye on the security of your job.

When your primary source of money is savings, you'll need to forecast how much you'll need to see you through the time it takes to complete your plan, or until your plan begins producing income.

And if you intend to finance your plan by borrowing money, you'll need to know about current interest rates, since any significant change can affect the cost of borrowing and, therefore, the cost of financing your plan.

These are just a few examples of how to ensure that you can get the inputs you need, when you need them, at the lowest costs. Now, what about *outputs*?

Outputs

The first thing you need to decide is *who* are you creating your outputs for? Whose *needs* are you trying to satisfy? This is very important, because he or she (or they) are your customers.

If, for example, your plan is to pursue a hobby, you're probably doing it for your own satisfaction, in which case your customer is *you*, and you're the only one you have to satisfy. You still have to rely on the outside world to get the *inputs* you need, but you already have a clear idea of what kind of *outputs* you expect.

But when you're trying to satisfy someone else's needs, you'll have the uncertainty of not knowing exactly what will please them.

Outputs can be classified into two categories: products and services.

A *product* is something tangible; something you can produce, see, and hold in your hand. Examples of products are cakes, toasters, books, and automobiles.

A *service*, on the other hand, is *intangible*; you don't produce it, you deliver it; and you can't necessarily see it or hold it in your hand. It's usually delivered directly to the customer, who is generally involved in the process. Examples of services are hairdressing, janitorial services, teaching, and delivery services.

You

As shown in Figure 1, *You* are the key to *everything*: to setting goals, acquiring inputs, and making sure that everything necessary to convert those inputs into outputs is done, and done *right*. And you'll have to rely on the things you do *well* – your strengths – to make it all happen. So it's important that you have a clear picture of your personal capabilities, as well as any other resources you have.

Your strengths are the things you do *best*, usually in the areas of knowledge, skills, and abilities, although some of your greatest strengths may also be your personal values, character, and reputation, all of which we'll discuss further in Chapter 14.

You'll need a clear picture of your strengths before you can build on them, and the best place to start is with your own opinion, since you know yourself better than anyone else does. List the things that *you* feel you're best at, which will probably include the things you *like* best, that *interest* you the most, and at which you've been the most *successful*. But that's just the beginning.

Next you should get opinions from others, because they can often see things about you that you can't. Which others? Anyone who *expect*s something of you or who is *affected* by what you do, which might include family, friends, and business associates. They are constantly analyzing what you're doing and how well you're doing it; and how well you're meeting their expectations (and they may even throw in a bonus: what they think are some of your *weaknesses*.)

Ask them to point out what they feel are your best points; your personal assets; your strengths.

Ask them "What do you see as my strengths, or potential strengths? What are your expectations of me? How do *you* measure my performance? What are the things that are most important to satisfying *your* expectations?"; then, "How well am I doing in each of those areas? Which do you see as my strengths? Where do I need to improve?"; and, finally, "How can I do a better job of meeting your expectations? What suggestions do you have that will help me better satisfy you?"

A different kind of problem faces people who don't think they *have* any strengths, even though nearly everyone does. Just because a person's strengths aren't obvious doesn't mean they don't have a special talent; something that can be developed into a strength, if it isn't one already. If you think this might be you—if

If Not Now, When?

you're not sure if you *have* any strengths, or not sure what they are—you may find it useful to take a look at Chapter 12, Self-Development..

Think of it this way: the world is full of people who do things well; people who are *good* at what they do. That's what most people expect of themselves, and of others: good work; good performance. But you can be better than good—you can be *exceptional*—and it doesn't take that much more. As we discussed earlier, you don't have to be smarter, or have exceptional talent; all it takes is doing a bit more—*exceeding* expectations—your own or those of others—and there's a simple formula for that.

First, you have to make sure you're always working on what's most *important*—your highest priority goals; and second, make sure you're always working at your highest level of *performance*. That's all it takes: work *harder* than the average person, and work on the *right* things. If you do that, and always *deliver a bit more than is expected,* you'll become an exceptional performer.

Needs

Once you have a clear picture of your strengths it's time to see if there's a difference, or gap, between where you *are* and where you *want* to be. This will show just how big a leap you'll have to make to get from here to there.

If there's something missing, something you *don't* have, you'll have two choices: 1) *get* whatever it is that you're missing; or 2) *change* your expectations (your goals) so they can be achieved *with* the resources you currently have. Some useful questions to consider are:

- What resources do I need to reach my goal? (e.g., skills, abilities, time, money, knowledge)
- Which of these resources do I currently have?
- Are there gaps—things I need but don't have?
- Can I get them by the time I'll need them?
- If so, what do I have to do?
- If not, how will it affect my ability to achieve the goal? (e.g., will it take longer; will I have to change the goal)

Resources

I don't know about you, but there are two things that I never seem to have enough of: time and money. It isn't that I'm destitute; it's just that there are so many things I want to do that I can't possibly do them all. So I have to make choices and, after I've made them, manage my time and money carefully to make sure there's enough of both to do the things that are most important to me. And that's what you should do: make sure you get the most from your resources; especially your time and money.

This means using your resources where they'll have the biggest impact on your plan; where they'll help achieve the goals that are most important. Since, like me, you may never have all of the resources you'd like,

If Not Now, When?

you'll have to make choices: *what* is most important to get done, and *when* (in what order.)

If you don't make those choices you may find yourself trying to do too many things at once, and not getting *any* of them done. So it's absolutely essential that you apply your resources to those activities that are most critical to your plan, even if it means delaying or postponing other pet projects.

Sometimes this will mean taking resources away from less important goals, to make sure they're available for those that are more important, and that's hard to do, especially when those goals are important, too. But if you don't do it, you won't get to where you want to go, and that's not the reason you bought this book, is it?

Resource allocation can be a powerful tool. If you reserve the resources for something, it *will* get done, and if you don't provide the resources, it *won't* get done. It's as simple as that; simple in concept, but not necessarily *easy*, because it's sometimes hard to maintain the self-discipline it takes stay on track—to say "no" and stick by our guns when we encounter resistance, or temptation.

Innovation

There's another important ability that we all have: our *creativity*; our ability to *innovate*. Although innovation is one of the most powerful capabilities we have, it's sort of a "secret weapon," because not many people think about it, realize they have it, or use it effectively. Perhaps they just don't see its importance, but it *is* important, because the more innovative, the more creative you are, the more you're willing to try new things, the more ways you'll find to be *better* at what you do, and the better you'll be able to chart your own future, rather than having it determined by someone else, or something else.

Innovation can be defined several ways, but it's basically the *first time* something is done, or the first time it's done in a *different* way. That means you don't have to be a genius to be innovative; you just have to push yourself to think differently, even to the point of being outrageous in the way you look at things.

Being innovative can be as simple as deliberately doing something in a way that is totally different than you had ever done it before, or looking at something from the *opposite* perspective. Innovation is sometimes referred to as "thinking outside the box," or "upside-down thinking," but no matter what it's called, it is a good way to get a different outlook.

As an example, for years I walked several miles each morning, generally following the same circular route in the same direction. One morning, for reasons I've since forgotten, I decided to walk the same route in the opposite direction, and was astonished at the difference. I saw a side of everything that I had never noticed before—buildings, ponds, trees, parks—and was amazed by how different everything looked. It was as though I was walking in another part of town.

You can try this yourself. Just reverse one of your normal routines, and see how different things look. Once you've convinced yourself how well it works,

If Not Now, When?

you'll find it easier to apply it to the way you make decisions. As you analyze a situation, first look at the solutions you would normally consider, then, before you make your decision, look at it from the opposite direction; from a contrarian perspective. You might be surprised at what you'll see that you might have otherwise overlooked.

And there's another way of getting different viewpoints: ask other people, especially people who think differently than you, and people who look at things in non-conventional ways. I've known people who even developed their own "board of directors", made up of those whose opinions they value; people with different backgrounds and experience. You might consider doing the same. Your "board" doesn't have to be large—two or three people will do—as long as they will be honest and direct in giving you their opinions. This can be a very effective way of broadening your perspective.

Innovation and creativity can be potent advantages. To become more innovative you need to think more outlandishly; make maximum use of your individuality, initiative, and creativity; and give yourself the opportunity to develop to your full potential.

The potential to be innovative resides in every one of us, so make sure you give yours the opportunity to flourish.

Summary

Ultimately, your long-term success will be affected by the way you anticipate and act on trends and events that happen in the outside world. When you have a clear window on the world you are better able to turn threats into opportunities and to be *proactive* in looking to the future, rather than *reacting* to whatever happens.

Although you can't *control* the outside world, there are many ways you can manage the way it affects your plan. You may not be able to predict the future, but you can spot trends that may someday affect you.

We've all seen businesses - there are lots of them - swept aside by changes they didn't see coming; yet just about every trend that brings major change is visible for a long time, often *years*, before it begins to affect us. These trends can be visible to anyone who makes it a point to look, but you won't see them if you don't look.

So make sure you *manage* your external world. Look for developing trends, decide whether they offer threats or opportunities for you, then act accordingly, *before* you're forced to. Here are several areas where you can look for trends; areas that tend to be major sources of the events and trends that affect us all:

- demographics
- education
- the workplace
- family issues
- government/legislation/politics
- the economy
- technology
- the physical environment
- globalization

CHAPTER 10 - <u>HOW'M I DOIN'?</u>

"The talent of success is nothing more than
doing what you can do well,
and doing well whatever you can do."
(Henry Wadsworth Longfellow, 1807-1882)

Well, you've finally reached the point you've been working toward: actually *doing* the things that will make your dream a reality. You're excited about it, and you *should* be. But just because you're putting your plan into action doesn't mean you're done planning; you're just beginning a new phase of it.

Your plan is just a place to start, and as you begin implementing it you'll find that some parts of it need to be changed, and that's just the beginning of a series of changes; a process that will continue until you've reached your goals.

As we discussed in the previous chapter, there's no way we can be certain what might happen in the future, but we can be *prepared* for whatever happens by observing trends in the world around us, and being ready to make changes, as we see the need. So, as you put your plan into action, you'll need to keep track of how well it's working, and when it needs to change; you'll need feedback.

Feedback
A plan is how we *intend* (hope) for things to happen, but it won't always work out the way we planned, and that's okay as long as we see anything that

goes wrong before it becomes a major problem, which means keeping a close eye on how well it's going, at all times.

It's fairly easy to evaluate how well a plan worked, *after* it's finished – when you've either reached your goals, or failed to reach them - but monitoring how well it's working while it's still in process is more difficult.

To do that, you'll need measurements for every activity in the plan, for the performance you *expect*.

In Chapter 5 we talked about setting goals – *measurable* goals – and Chapter 6 discussed how to develop the action plans to reach those goals. So, if you've done that, you already know how you'll measure your *expected* performance. As a reminder, you determined those measurements by answering three questions for each action or outcome:

1. *What* action, activity, or outcome are you measuring?
2. *How much* of it do you *expect* to achieve? (what quantity)
3. *By when* (what date, time) do you expect to achieve it?

But you also need to measure your *actual* performance, so you can compare it against the performance you had *expected* at each stage of the plan. This will let you know how you're doing at any stage of the implementation process. *Actual* performance can be measured by answering three similar questions:

If Not Now, When?

1. *What* action, activity, or outcome are you measuring?
2. *How much* of it have you achieved, so far? (what quantity)
3. *How* much had you *expected* to achieve by this time? (what quantity)

To get the most accurate view of how you're doing, you'll have to monitor actions or outcomes in at least three areas: inputs, outputs, and the process you use to turn inputs into outputs.

Outputs, of course, are the final measure of performance but, as we discussed earlier, in most cases they can't be measured until after you're done, which is too late; you need to know how you're doing *while* you're still doing it.

That begins with keeping track of your *inputs*, to make sure you have the materials, information, and equipment you need, when you need them.

Then you can evaluate the *transformation* process – your actions; the things that *you* do - so you can spot and correct minor nuisances before they become major problems. Does any good cook ever finish a dish without, in some way, testing the quality of the process (e.g., tasting it) while he's fixing it? Or does any serious student wait until a course is over to determine how she's doing? Of course not.

Evaluation has to be honest and objective, and should include assessing how *you* think you're doing and what you think might need to be done better, or differently. You may find, for instance, that you need knowledge, skills, or abilities that you don't currently have.

By continuously monitoring how you're doing, you'll be making sure your final outputs will be what you expected them to be.

The most important thing to remember is that measuring performance is of little value unless you use it to *improve* performance; to find ways to do things better. That requires a clear idea of *what* you intend to measure, and *how* you plan to measure it.

If you do that, you'll always be able to see where your plan is working and where it isn't, and you can change it accordingly, when and where it's necessary. This has two major benefits: 1) it makes the plan dynamic – constantly evolving; always improving; and 2) it enables you to learn from your experience.

But don't forget, there are others who may also measure your performance. We call them *stakeholders*.

Stakeholders

Those who are important to our success - people, groups, and organizations – usually have something to gain or lose from our actions. They are affected by what we do or how we do it, and have different, sometimes conflicting, opinions about our results. And they have different ways of showing their pleasure or displeasure, and of influencing us accordingly. So, it's important to ask yourself:

- Who are my most important stakeholders?

- Why are *they* important to me?
- How do they influence me?
- What do I need from them?
    - Why am *I* important to them?
    - What do they expect of me?
    - What criteria do they use to measure my performance?
    - How well am I meeting their expectations?
- What can I do to satisfy them better?

Examples of stakeholders and their expectations include:

Stakeholder	Expectations
Family	Safety, security, love, companionship, understanding
Friends	Friendship, companionship, loyalty, shared interests
Customers	Value, dependability, reliability, consistency
Co-workers	Collegiality, cooperation, support
Employer	Loyalty, enthusiasm, hard work
Yourself	Needs, desires, dreams, aspirations

And I'm sure you realize that, with so many conflicting expectations, it will be almost impossible to satisfy *everyone*, but here's what you *can* do.

Decide who are your most *important* stakeholders, and make sure you understand what they expect of you.

Usually they will be the ones who have the most influence over you: those who can provide the greatest rewards or the most severe punishment, or both, like your boss, or your family, friends, and co-workers.

You should *consider* their opinions, but never forget: your first responsibility is to meet *your own* expectations.

Summary

When we don't know how we're doing, it's like being lost on a country road: if we don't know where we *are*, how will we know which way to go to get where we're *going*?

To reach your goals, you need feedback: information that helps you know where you *are* at all times, and lets you compare that with where you had *planned* to be at those times. Feedback is an important part of performance evaluation. In implementing a plan, as in traveling, we reach our goals by knowing where we are, how we're doing, and making changes when they're necessary.

So you need a measurement system that will give you a constant flow of information about how you're doing. With that, you can compare your actual performance with the performance you had planned, and make whatever changes are necessary to make sure your plan stays on course.

CHAPTER 11 - <u>CHANGING</u>

"Nothing endures but change."
(Heraclitus, 540-480 BC)

The world around us is constantly changing, and affecting the way we live and work. We have three choices about change: we can *lead* change, *resist* it, or try to *influence* how it affects us. The choice we make will depend on how we feel about change: does it threaten or challenge us?

We've already discussed the third option – *influencing* change – in Chapter 9, so now we'll concentrate on the other two: *leading* change, and *resisting* it, and their advantages and disadvantages.

Resisting Change

When faced with change, why is our first reaction so often to resist? Robbins (1993) tells us the most common reasons are:

1. *Habit* - we get used to doing things a certain way and resist changing our habits;
2. *Security* - we feel safer in a familiar situation than in a new and uncertain one;
3. *Economic* - concern that the change will affect our income;
4. Fear of the *unknown* - what we know, even if we don't particularly like it, is less threatening than what we *don't* know;

If Not Now, When?

5. *Selective information-processing* – we hear what we want to hear, and we interpret what we hear by our own experience and perceptions.

You may have noticed a common thread among those concerns: uncertainty. Any change causes some uncertainty which, as we've previously discussed, makes us uncomfortable. We relish the comfort of what we *know*, so we prefer things that are familiar to those that are new, or to those we're not sure about. Most of us become accustomed to working and living in "comfortable ruts," and until our situation becomes unbearable, we prefer to stay right here, thank you.

Inertia, you'll recall, is that invisible force that makes it easier to keep doing what we're doing than to do something different. I point this out because a lot of our tendency to resist change is caused by a combination of uncertainty and inertia.

And I'll add one more reason we resist change, one that has nothing to do with uncertainty: *overconfidence*. Long-term success carries with it an increasing risk of overconfidence, sometimes even *arrogance*. The longer we're successful at something, and the more successful we are, the more confident we become that we'll *always* be successful.

This attitude may contribute to the popular saying, "If it ain't broke, don't fix it" which, in my mind, is just a way of closing our eyes (and minds) to the need for change. So we should also consider an entirely different perspective – that success breeds failure -

which suggests that a changing world doesn't necessarily respect past success.

With so many reasons to be threatened by change, it's no wonder we're more inclined to resist it than to welcome it. And resisting isn't always bad. Some resistance can provide a stability that makes us less likely to be jerked around by uncertainty, fads, or indecisive decision-making.

But people, even those who are highly resistant to change, can often be influenced to change if it's proposed in the right way. While we may not respond to *arbitrary* or *impulsive* attempts, we can often be convinced by a deliberate well-thought-out analysis of *why* the change is necessary.

However, resistance can be bad when it's so deeply entrenched it makes us resist to the point that we become pawns of the outside world and its uncertainties. When that happens, we're letting our destiny be determined by *someone else* or *something else*, sometimes with painful consequences. That's a major difference between planned and unplanned change.

Planned change is *deliberate* – it's change that *we* create – and it's generally done well in advance of when it's needed, on our terms and our timetable. *Unplanned* change happens when we don't see it coming, and it creates a crisis that *forces* us to change.

Although we all face crises from time to time, the way we deal with them can have markedly different outcomes. Those who manage according to a deliberate plan are much more likely to anticipate the need for change, plan for it, and introduce change *before* it's forced on them, thereby *preventing* a crisis. Those who *don't* plan are likely to delay acting until after the situation becomes *critical*, then *react* to a set of circumstances over which they have little or no control.

Leading Change

Those who make a conscious decision to *lead* change, rather than being led by it, will invariably find more *opportunities* in the world around them, while those who resist change will see more *threats*.

As a result, our success can be dramatically affected by how responsive we are in changing, developing, and improving. It's been said that if we're not moving forward we might well be moving backward, and there's no question that the more turbulent the outside world, the more dynamic we have to be, just to keep up. The leaders in any field are usually those who have decided to *lead* change rather than resist it.

Our attitude toward change is strongly influenced by how clearly we understand *why* change is necessary, and what advantages it offers. A genuine understanding of change requires understanding the answers to five questions:

1. *What* is driving the change?
2. *Who* is initiating the change?
3. *What* must be changed?
4. *How* will the change be accomplished?
5. *When* will the change take place?

What is driving change? Although there are many possibilities, some of the more common drivers are changes in:

- *technology* - new technology can change how we do things, and the skills and capabilities we need to do them;
- *environment* - when the outside world changes, it changes the issues we deal with and how we deal with them.

Who is initiating the change? In organizations, change is most often initiated by executives, managers, or specialists/consultants who are called in as advisors. In these situations, trust has a major influence on our attitude toward change; how strongly we support or resist it depends on how legitimate we feel the reasons for the change are.

But when *you're* the one who's thinking about making a change, *you* will decide whether or not to change, when to change, and how to change. Although outside forces may be driving the need to change, the decision to change or not change is *yours* alone.

What must be changed? Is it your attitude, your goals, how you do things, or the way you allocate resources? If it's about how you *do* things, you may have to learn new skills, capabilities, or expertise to prepare for the future.

When the change takes place will be determined by two issues: 1) when does it *need* to be done? (i.e., Is there a deadline?); and 2) *how* will it be done? To a

If Not Now, When?

great extent, the method you use will determine what things must happen, and when they need to happen.

Deciding *how* to activate change begins with a choice between doing it incrementally, or radically.

Incremental change is gradual change, a little at a time, step-by-step, in a non-threatening manner. When you see the need to change well in advance of when it is necessary, you can do it in small bites, rather than swallowing it whole, which makes it less threatening, and more acceptable to those affected.

Radical change happens all at once, and often becomes necessary when you've delayed changing until there's a crisis, then have to do it all at once, in a sudden *reaction*, rather than a carefully-planned action.

Whether you make change incrementally or in large steps isn't as important as deciding to change in the first place. It's much better to *choose* to change, than to wait until you're *forced* to. And the best way to make sure you change by choice, rather than by chance, is to see the need for change well in advance, then make it happen on *your* terms.

Summary

Since the world around us is constantly changing, our success depends on how we respond to it. We *know* that change will come; we just don't know what it will be, or when, or where, or how. But watching trends will allow us to see things that are likely to affect us, as they develop – before they actually affect us. When we see them coming we can begin making small changes well in advance, and reduce the probability of suddenly having to face a crisis.

So, when it comes right down to it, you have two choices: take charge of your own destiny or leave it to chance. Which makes the most sense to you?

PART IV

BECOMING

The most important part of your plan for success is *you*; what you are now, and what you want to be—the *you* that will take you where you want to go.

The chapters in this section are all about *self-development,* including examining who you are - your likes and dislikes - what you're good at, and how to set personal goals, to become what and who you want to be.

The last chapter asks you to look into the future and picture how you'd like your life to look when someday you look back on it.

CHAPTER 12 – SELF-<u>DEVELOPMENT</u>

> "This above all: to thine own self be true,
> and it must follow, as the night the day,
> that thou canst not then be false to any man."
> (William Shakespeare, 1564-1616)

As we discussed earlier, for many years we were able to depend on our employers for job security, but not anymore. Now, some of the largest, most powerful companies in the world are laying off thousands of people; people who believed they had lifetime job security.

By now it should be clear to all of us that we can't depend on someone else for our security; we have to take responsibility for it ourselves. Our only real job security will come from the value of our abilities, skills, and knowledge.

This means that personal development is more important than ever. It's up to each of us to make sure we have the capabilities to keep pace with the changing needs of the world in which we work and live. And that's an *individual* process, because your development needs, and mine, are different from everyone else's.

Although it sometimes seems like we spend most of our time responding to *everyone else's* demands, that isn't the way it *should* be. *Your* needs should drive your desires, ambitions, and interests.

While it's ok to feel obligated to others, you shouldn't let those obligations overshadow your responsibilities to yourself. We've talked about this before, so you know how I feel about it: you owe it to yourself to pursue *your* dreams; they're at least as important as any other obligations you may feel.

But you should also recognize that your interests and ambitions may not always be the same as they are today. They're likely to change over the span of your life and, as they do, your self-development needs will also change.

It's been said that we go through as many as six different stages in our working careers:

1. preparation for work   (0-25)
2. organizational entry   (18-25)
3. early career   (25-40)
4. mid career   (40-55)
5. late career   (55-retirement)
6. retirement

If that's true, our interests, ambitions, and desires may also change that often.

No matter which stage of your life you're planning right now, a well thought-out development plan can be helpful. I recommend a three-stage process: self-assessment, setting goals, and job identification.

Self-Assessment
The purpose of self-assessment is to gain a clear understanding of your interests, ambitions, desires, and values, as well as your skills and abilities. We've talked about this before, but this time I want you to go

through a more detailed process, beginning with a look at some of the things that are likely to have the strongest influence on you:

Internal Influences

- your desires/ambitions - what you hope to achieve
- your interests - what fascinates/intrigues you
  - what you enjoy doing
- your values - the ones that are most important to you
- your academic aptitudes and achievements
- your occupational aptitudes and skills
- your communication skills/abilities
- your social skills

External Influences

- your family's values and expectations
- economic conditions
- employment trends
- the job market
- long-term employment opportunities

Once you've thought about the things that are most likely to influence you, you should answer the following questions:

a. What are my most important personal characteristics?
   (e.g., dependability, intelligence, interpersonal skills)

b. What managerial or leadership skills and abilities do I have?
   (e.g., organization, problem-solving, conflict management)
c. What other job-related capabilities do I have?
   (e.g., computer skills, mathematics, writing ability)
d. What are my most important work-related accomplishments?
   (e.g., improved work methods, increased sales, reduced costs)
e. On what job factors have I received the highest performance evaluations (or the most frequent compliments)?
   (e.g., quality, productivity, dependability, innovation)
f. What recognition/awards have I received, outside of work?
   (e.g., church work, volunteer work, teaching, mentoring)
g. What are my favorite interests/hobbies?
   (e.g., music, woodworking, sports, art)

Setting Goals

Now you're ready to set some self-development goals; goals that will ensure that you balance your workplace ambitions – what you *have* to do - with your personal desires – what you *like* to do. Of course if you don't have a job, or don't need a job, you can focus entirely on what you enjoy. In either case, here are four questions to help you get started:

1. What is my most important goal?
2. What's the first thing I need to do to reach it?
   2a. What additional steps will I need to take, and in what order?
3. Are there any skills or knowledge that I need but don't have?
   3a. What steps do I need to take to develop them, and in what order?
4. What kinds of help, advice, guidance will I need, to achieve my goals?
   4a. Where can I get it?

Remember, although it's possible to work on more than one goal at a time, you will be more likely to achieve your goals by focusing on them one at a time.

Here are some additional questions that can be helpful in goal-setting:

a. What are my long-term personal/family goals?
   (e.g., desired standard of living, location, flexibility)
b. What interests or activities would I like to pursue?
   (e.g., volunteer work, outdoor activities, travel)
c. What kind of balance would I like to achieve between my job obligations and personal goals?

Job Identification

If you're one of those people who (like me) still *has* to work for a living (or if you just *prefer* to work,) your next assignment is to identify the types of jobs/careers that match your desires, ambitions, interests and, where possible, your knowledge, skills, and abilities. Questions that may be helpful:

a. What types of work interest me?
b. Am I things-oriented, or people-oriented?
c. What kinds of work make me feel most worthwhile?
   (e.g., helping others, or developing new products)
d. What rewards do I want from my job?
   (e.g., money, job security, recognition, satisfaction)
e. How much job freedom do I want?
   (e.g., autonomy, or close supervision)
f. What are five characteristics of my ideal job?
   (e.g., flexible hours, work from home, autonomy)
g. What would be the best kind of organization for me?
   (e.g., size, location, products/services, reputation, value-system, culture)
h. What are my career goals?
   How well do they match my job/career choices?

Although there are many commercially-available tests that match personal characteristics and interests with various types of jobs, here are three that I've found particularly useful. Any one of them can help you get a better idea of which types of jobs/careers would best suit you:

- the *Campbell Interest and Skill Survey*, at
   http://www.pearsonassessments.com/tests/ciss.htm

- the Career Cruiser, at
   http://www.careercruising.com

- the *Strong Interest Inventory*, at
  http://www.personalitydesk.com

Although these sources charge a nominal fee (usually less than $100,) they are often available free of charge through career centers at community colleges and state universities.

Summary

Self-assessment, goal-setting, and job identification are the keys to a successful career development plan; one that will increase your future security, as well as your personal satisfaction.

An ongoing self-development program will keep you abreast of what's going on in your areas of interest, including the availability of current jobs, and future job prospects. But most important, it will help you keep in touch with yourself: your own desires, ambitions, and interests, as they evolve and change throughout your life.

CHAPTER 13 - LEARNING

"There is only one good, knowledge,
and one evil, ignorance."
(Socrates, 439-399 B.C.)

Learning is how we get new knowledge, get better at what we do, and grow.

Knowledge
People have always sought knowledge for two reasons: for practical purposes, to become more effective (e.g., to know how to read, write, speak, and *do* things); and for personal reasons, to understand ourselves, so we can grow (e.g., intellectually, morally, or spiritually.)

Each of us has two types of knowledge: explicit knowledge and implicit knowledge.

Explicit knowledge is the things we know that can be written down, recorded, and taught. It's knowledge that we can easily pass on to others, and program into computers.

Implicit knowledge, on the other hand, exists only in our memories, our intuition, our judgment, and the rules of thumb we develop through experience. Sometimes referred to as *tacit* knowledge, it includes creative ideas and solutions that are often difficult to explain to others, because we may not understand them ourselves.

If Not Now, When?

Anyone, for example, can bake a cake by following a recipe – *explicit* knowledge passed on through a set of instructions. But prize-winning cakes take more than a recipe. They are created by people who, through practice, have developed *implicit* knowledge. They've learned that special taste comes from a pinch of this, a dollop of that, and frequent sampling. That kind of knowledge isn't included in a recipe; it only comes from experience.

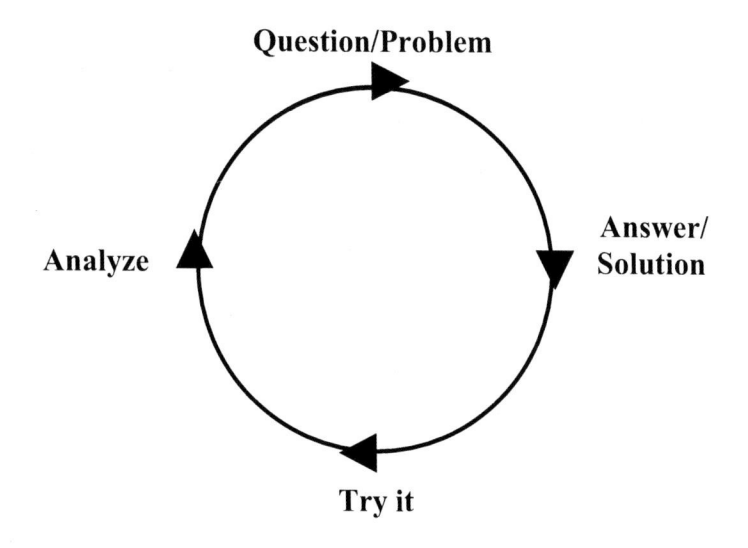

Figure 2. How We Learn

Learning

We get both explicit and implicit knowledge through learning, a circular process which, as shown in Figure 2, always begins with a problem or question.

Once we have a clear idea of a problem, we normally start thinking about how to solve it. We consider possible solutions, select the one that looks best, and try it to see how well it works. After trying it, we analyze how it went: did it work the way we thought it would? If not, what went wrong? Then we start the process all over again: we look at the problem again, come up with another idea, and try it. And we keep circling through this process until we find something that works.

This should sound familiar; it's probably the way you learned a lot of what you know. Think, for example, about how you learned to read, write, and do arithmetic. You probably read about it, had it explained to you, then practiced it over and over. Although most of what you learned that way was explicit knowledge, practicing made you better at it, by adding *implicit* knowledge.

Although we can learn a lot by listening and watching, some things can only be learned by *doing*: by trying, analyzing how we did, then trying again. Perhaps the most valuable part of learning-by-doing is the experience we get that makes us better problem solvers.

How did you learn to walk, for example, or ride a bicycle, drive a car, or hit a golf ball? Were you able to do it right, after somebody explained it to you? Probably not. Although they could tell you what to do and how to do it, that wasn't enough. Sure, it helped you understand what you were *supposed* to do, but you had to learn the rest of it yourself, through trial and error: by trying, failing, and trying again.

Understanding how we learn should give us a better idea of what learning *is*, and what it *isn't*.

Learning is *not* memorizing, or knowing the answers, and it *isn't* only about learning from others. Some things we have to learn for ourselves, and those are often our most valuable experiences.

Learning *is* about questioning, thinking, testing, evaluating, and improving. It *is* about trying, and sometimes failing. It *is* about persistence and commitment, and it *is* a big part of how we grow.

It's important to remember that a lot of your most valuable knowledge may only exist in your memories, and sometimes only in your subconscious memory. Yet it may be some of the most valuable knowledge you have, because it's the kind that can make you really good at what you do. When we enjoy doing something we keep working to get better at it. The more we try the better we get, and that's what makes each of us unique.

Summary

Learning shouldn't be something we only do while we're young, or while we're still in school; it should be continuous, a lifelong thing. We build on the knowledge we have by:

- retaining it, using it, keeping it active,
- acquiring new information,
- learning through new experiences.

Retaining knowledge is how we write our history. Remembering what we've done, why we did it, and what worked and what didn't, are all essential to making sure that we learn from our experience; that we don't waste time repeating something we've already done, and that we don't make the same mistake twice.

> "Those who cannot remember the past
> are condemned to repeat it."
> (George Santayana, 1863-1952)

The way to become exceptional is to keep learning; keep trying to find better ways to do what you do; keep learning from the things you try, and gaining from your experiences. Sure, you'll fail now and then, but that's okay. Failure is an important part of growing. When we fail, it's usually because we're trying something new, something different, so it really isn't failure, at all; it's gaining experience, and *learning* in the process.

CHAPTER 14 - <u>CHARACTER</u> & VALUES

"Associate yourself with men of quality
if you esteem your own reputation,
for 'tis better to be alone than in bad company."
(George Washington, 1732-1799)

Character

Most of us, either consciously or unconsciously, separate the people we know into two categories: those we can trust and those we can't, and the difference has a lot to do with their character.

The dictionary defines character as "The moral or ethical structure of a person..."

Character is built on values; the values that guide our behavior, the decisions we make, and our actions.

Our character is developed either by choice or chance. We can *choose* what kind of person we want to be, or we can just let our character develop on its own.

When a person's character develops on its own, it may be because he didn't think character was important, or that he just never thought about it. But we *should* think about it, because our values, or lack of values, influence every part of our lives, everything that we do and, perhaps most important, whether or not others trust us.

People with good character usually have strong, positive, value systems, and their decisions and actions are based on those values; values that give them a good sense of right and wrong.

But when character evolves on its own, it's likely to take the easiest route – the path of least resistance – and be based on whatever is most important to *others*, and what will make us popular with them. People with this kind of character are likely to base their behavior on what everyone else is doing, regardless of whether it's right or wrong. After all, how wrong can it be if everyone else is doing it?

But the fact that a lot of people are doing something doesn't make it right. In fact, what's *right* (i.e., *morally* right) is often just the opposite of what most people are doing, because so many people choose whatever is *easiest*, and not necessarily what is *right*.

We can only build and reinforce a strong character by being true to ourselves and to what *we* believe in, no matter what anyone else thinks, or does. The decisions we make and the actions we take should be true to *our* character and *our* values, and the more we stick to what we believe in, the more firm we'll become in those convictions.

> "Sow a thought and you reap an act;
> Sow an act and you reap a habit;
> Sow a habit and you reap a character;
> Sow a character and you reap a destiny."
> (Samuel Smiles, 1812-1904)

Ethics

People of character let their values guide their decisions, and they have a strong sense of responsibility to everyone who is, or will be, affected by their actions.

If Not Now, When?

Their decisions and actions are guided by *moral* standards; not by convenience, opportunism, or self interest.

A sense of responsibility is the foundation of *ethics*: the rules and standards that govern our conduct. Our personal codes of ethics are based on how willing we are to accept responsibility and accountability for our actions, and to recognize and respect the rights of others. Acting ethically sounds simple and it is, in principle, but that doesn't mean it's *easy*. Living by our values is sometimes difficult, and the rewards aren't always immediate, but we do it because we believe it will ultimately pay off.

> "When the one great scorer comes to write against your name – he marks – not that you won or lost – but how you played the game."
> (Grantland Rice, 1880-1954)

Values

The dictionary defines a value as, "A principle, standard, or quality considered inherently worthwhile or desirable." Rokeach (1973) describes value as "a belief that one type of conduct is preferable to the opposite type of conduct," which is another way of saying that our values influence our behavior by helping us distinguish right from wrong.

While some people have very strongly-held values, others don't think much about their values, so their actions may be influenced more by circumstances than by any thought about what's right or wrong.

Those with strong values know what they believe in and where they're going. They know who they are and what they stand for, while those without a clear sense of values tend to be influenced by the philosophies of those around them; philosophies like "if it feels good, do it."

People with strong values take responsibility for their actions, control what they do, and influence what happens to them, while those without strong values are more likely to be influenced by what *other* people think and do.

When you have a strong sense of your values, you always have a point of reference; you can easily determine when somebody else's values or the values of an organization don't agree with yours, and act accordingly.

Values give meaning to what we do. They influence our attitudes, shape our behaviors, are instrumental in which dreams and visions we pursue, and guide us in developing our personal plans for achieving our dreams. A strong value system and a positive, deliberately-developed character is the path to personal credibility and an enviable reputation.

Your values, along with your background and experience, are what define your unique character. Your character, in turn, guides your commitment to beliefs and values that are even larger than your own. Character influences how we do everything that we do: how we process information and make decisions, and how we interpret and manage the world around us.

If Not Now, When?

Developing the kind of character you want requires a strong personal commitment, but once you've done it, maintaining it will become easier and easier as your pride in the person you're becoming gets stronger and stronger.

Summary
Your character can have a major influence on your success or failure. You *will* develop some type of character, whether you do it deliberately or just let it happen. But if you let it evolve on its own, it is much less likely to be an asset than if you make a conscious effort to develop the character you *want*.

Your character is based on the values that are most important to you; values that guide your behavior. Since it has a powerful influence on your behavior, character can be a strong deterrent to improper or unacceptable behavior. Your character defines your attitude, and is a constant reminder of your values, beliefs and responsibilities.

Good character is build on values like honesty, integrity, loyalty and trust, to name just a few. We nurture and maintain character through our daily activities – by constantly *practicing* what we believe in – and *our* actions can set a powerful example for others. In this sense, *what* we do and *how* we do it sends a much clearer message of our values and beliefs than anything we could possibly *say*.

> "What you are stands over you the while, and thunders so that I cannot hear what you say to the contrary."
>
> (Ralph Waldo Emerson, 1803-1882)

Today, organizations are becoming more dependent on knowledge and less on manual labor. They expect the people they hire to take responsibility for their own actions: for how, where, and when they do their jobs.

They hire people they can depend on; people they can trust; people with character. They no longer try to control *how* people work as closely as they once did. They depend, instead, on the values, beliefs, and understood practices of people of good character.

Make sure you're one of *those* people.

CHAPTER 15 - **LOOKING BACK**

"I think the purpose of life is to be useful,
to be responsible,
to be compassionate.
It is, above all, to matter:
to count,
to stand for something,
to have made some difference that you lived at all."
(Leo Rosten, 1908-1997)

A minister asked the members of his congregation to look forward to the end of their lives and try to imagine what their friends, neighbors, and co-workers would say about them at the funeral. The idea, of course, was to get people to reflect on how they're living their lives and to think about what they should be doing *now* that will let them look back on their lives with pride and satisfaction.

I've thought a lot about what he said, and how it applies to me. It's a sobering thought: what *do* people think of me, about how I'm living my life, and how it affects *them*? Even more important, "How do *I* feel about the way I'm spending my life?"

Now I'm asking you to think about that, and ask yourself "When I look back, how will I feel about the way I spent *my* life?"

If you learned that you were going to die tomorrow, how would you feel about what you've done with your life so far? What have you done that you had intended to do? And even more important, what *haven't* you done that you want to do? Regardless of how you answer those questions, you should consider yourself lucky, because the odds are that you *won't* die tomorrow, or the next day. You're *not* at the end of your life; in fact, as you've heard so many times, *today is the first day of the rest of your life.*

It isn't too late; it's *never* too late, so why not take steps now to make sure you'll be satisfied with the way you lived your life? What you've done in the past, or left undone, doesn't really matter; what's important is what you do from now on. And don't try to hide behind that lame excuse, "I'm too old. It's too late for me." That's nonsense! It doesn't matter how old you are, you can still do it.

> "It's never too late to be what you might have been."
>
> (George Eliot, 1819-1880)

You're never going to be any younger than you are right now, so don't waste any more time. Sit down, right now, and picture the rest of your life as you would like to live it, encouraged by this thought:

> "If one advances confidently in the direction of his dreams, and endeavors to live the life which he has imagined, he will meet with a success unexpected in common hours."
>
> (Henry David Thoreau, 1817-1862)

In closing, I hope I've convinced you that you *should* follow your dreams; that you can do anything you *believe* you can do; and that by following the step-by-step process outlined in this book, you know *how* to do it. So why wait any longer? Get going! After all, if you don't do it now, when *will* you do it?

If not now, when?

REFERENCES

Bach, R.D., 1970, *Jonathon Livingston Seagull,* New York: Avon Books

Bluedorn, A.C., 2002, *The Human Organization of Time*, Stanford, CA: Stanford University Press

Bristol, C.M., 1948, *The Magic of Believing*, New York: Simon & Schuster

Carnegie, D., 1962, *The Quick and Easy Way to Effective Speaking*, New York: Association Press

Longaberger, D., 2001, *Longaberger: An American Success Story*, New York: Harper Business

Maslow, A.H., 1998, *Maslow on Management*, New York: John Wiley & Sons.

Peale, N.V., 1952, *The Power of Positive Thinking*, New York: Ballantine Books

Robbins, J.R., 1993, *Organization Theory: Structure, Design, and Applications*, Englewood Cliffs, NJ: Prentice Hall

Rokeach, M., 1973, *The Nature of Human Values*, New York: The Free Press